AMUNDSEN'S
WAY

Also by Joanna Grochowicz

Into the White

AMUNDSEN'S
WAY

THE RACE TO
THE SOUTH POLE

JOANNA GROCHOWICZ

ALLEN&UNWIN
SYDNEY • MELBOURNE • AUCKLAND • LONDON

Allen & Unwin
83 Alexander Street
Crows Nest NSW 2065
Australia
Phone: (61 2) 8425 0100
Email: info@allenandunwin.com
Web: www.allenandunwin.com

A catalogue record for this book is available from the National Library of Australia

ISBN 978 1 76063 766 8

For teaching resources, explore
www.allenandunwin.com/resources/for-teachers

Cover and text design by Joanna Hunt
Cover and text illustrations by Sarah Lippett
Set in 11/17.5 pt ITC Legacy Serif by Midland Typesetters, Australia

Printed in Australia in January 2020 by Griffin Press, Part of Ovato

10 9 8 7 6 5 4 3 2

www.joannagrochowicz.com

The paper in this book is FSC® certified. FSC® promotes environmentally responsible, socially beneficial and economically viable management of the world's forests.

For Dad

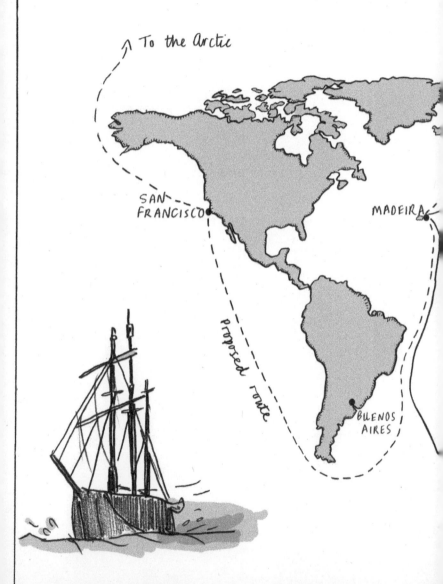

ACTUAL JOURNEY
PROPOSED JOURNEY

To the Arctic

SAN FRANCISCO

MADEIRA

Proposed route

BUENOS AIRES

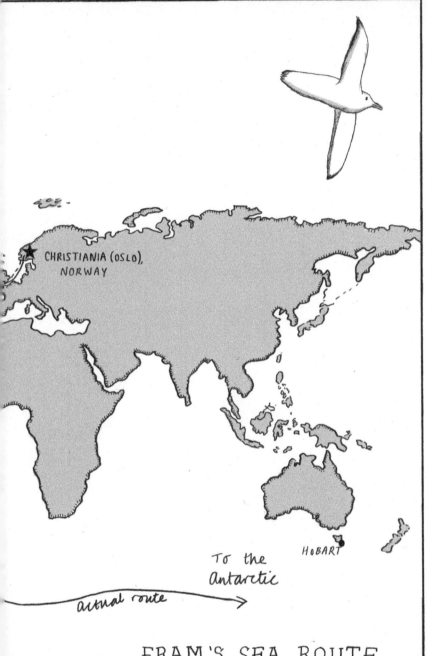

CHRISTIANIA (OSLO), NORWAY

HOBART

To the Antarctic

actual route →

FRAM'S SEA ROUTE

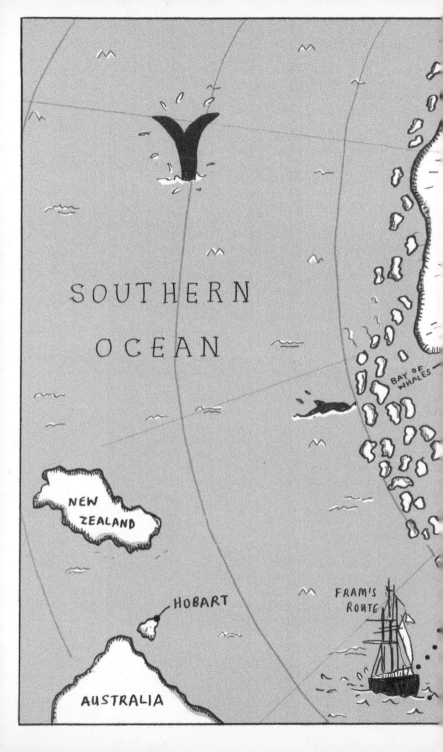

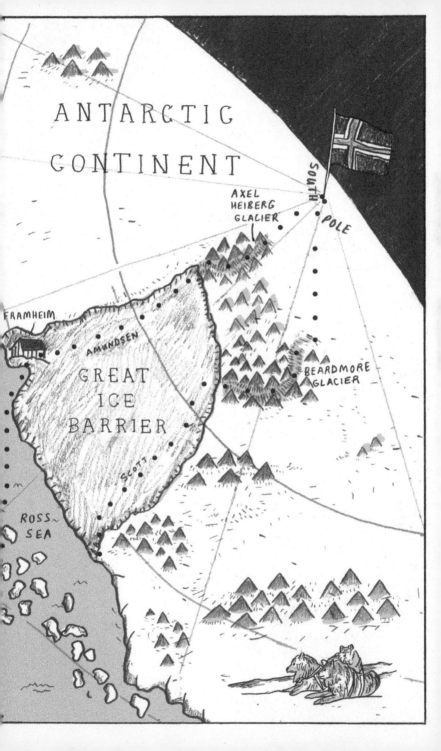

Oscar Wisting

Helmer Hansen

Olav Bjaaland

Sverre Hassel

7 MARCH 1912 – HOBART

Many years from now, the people of Hobart will tell how he strode up Murray Street, an imposing figure flanked by two fearsome sledge dogs. But this is not the case. On this particular Thursday morning, Roald Amundsen is just a man heading up the hill to Hadley's Orient Hotel, completely alone and in possession of news that will soon echo around the world.

Sledge dogs are far from his thoughts. Neither is he concerned about what his crew are doing aboard the *Fram*, which has dropped anchor in the middle of the Derwent River. One clear thought spurs him on – hot water.

He imagines soap and steam and how it will feel to slide his weary explorer's body into an extravagantly deep bath. A proper wash in a proper bathroom; he can think of no greater luxury. It's been a year and a half.

Needless to say, Amundsen is not a fetching sight. In his filthy old cap and an ancient blue jersey riddled with holes, he appears more tramp than polar hero. Pedestrians alter their pace; some slow to let him pass, others pull their children aside. Amundsen sees the wrinkled-up noses, the odd looks at his attire. He cares little. Anonymity comes as a relief. He's not ready for people. Not quite yet.

To a man so used to walking on snow, the sensation of paving stones underfoot is unnerving. So too the loud, clacking sounds of the port, the swish of soft skirts, the peaty scent of horse manure on cobbles warmed by the sun.

It was cooler on the water. The town seems airless by comparison. Sweaty, irritable, the explorer finds fault with the bustle of the place, the very squareness of the buildings. Even the air, flecked with dust, is disagreeable, filling his mouth with too much flavour. Coughing repeatedly, he longs to fill his lungs with a clean breeze off the sea, to feel the satisfying pang of air as cold as ice.

Hadley's Orient Hotel is a grand institution, judging by the white columns flanking its entry. Perhaps that's why the harbourmaster so eagerly recommended it. Amundsen grasps the brass handrail like a lifeline and hefts himself up the stairs and into the hotel's richly decorated lobby. The feeling of carpet is like a revelation; the deep red pattern is so intense it makes his eyes swim. Perhaps this moment, this return to the civilised world of man, marks the end of his journey. The thought is not altogether pleasing. In fact the ill-humour Amundsen has been nursing since stepping ashore has coalesced into a hard knot at the back of his throat and refuses to budge. How he longs for hot water.

The young clerk regards with an insolent expression the tall, unkempt individual standing at the front desk.

Amundsen clears his throat. 'A room. With bathroom.' It's been so long since he spoke English that the words come out gruff and mangled.

'I'm sorry, I can't understand you,' the clerk says, failing to make any effort.

Amundsen tenses his jaw and resists the urge to bring his fist down on the counter. Instead he tries again with greater care. Several other guests have gathered behind him. A lady in a large hat brings a handkerchief to her nose.

'I'm sorry. I'll have to get the manager,' says the clerk, unsure of how to proceed with dignity.

When the manager arrives he's taken off guard. They're not used to such people in their establishment.

'Can I help you?' His manner is brisk, designed to move this undesirable person along.

'Yes. A room with bathroom,' Amundsen repeats slowly.

'Do you have a reservation?'

Amundsen shakes his head and shifts his weight.

'We are rather full, I'm afraid.'

The young clerk looks over the register, his eyes flicking up at the manager.

'Ah yes, we can offer . . . a room.' The manager glances at the other people waiting and hurriedly points to the spot on the page where Amundsen is to leave his signature, although he doubts this man can even write.

It's not far to walk, just along the hall at the rear of the building, where he finds a door below a flight of stairs. The room is dark and there's a narrow, stained mattress on one wall and a bucket and mop propped against the other. The only window gives onto an alleyway strewn with broken crates and other rubbish. There is no bath. Just a chipped basin with grubby cake of soap stuck to its lip.

When Amundsen returns to the front desk a few minutes later, a cool manner disguises the fire burning in his chest. He is ready for battle.

'Amundsen!'

A well-dressed, barrel-chested man extends his arm in anticipation of a handshake. 'Allow me to introduce myself: James Macfarlane, Norwegian consul, at your service!'

Amundsen takes Macfarlane's hand, a little confused.

'The harbourmaster's been in touch. He told me he sent you up to Hadley's to freshen up – I came as quick as I could.'

It's unclear who is more surprised, Amundsen, the hotel manager or the terrified looking clerk who knows he's about to get into trouble.

'I trust you've been given the full treatment,' Macfarlane says. 'Something befitting a world-famous explorer who has just returned from more than a year in Antarctica.'

Amundsen arches one eyebrow, which sends the hotel manager into a frenzy of key rattling. 'There's been a terrible mix-up with my clerk,' he babbles. 'He gave you the wrong room. In fact, we have you staying in our suite. Top floor, sir. Shall I send the bellboy to help you with your luggage?'

Amundsen turns from the manager and instead addresses Macfarlane. 'A pleasure to meet with you. Thank you for coming. I have many important arrangements to make, telegrams to send.'

Macfarlane nods. 'You would like to send word of your safe return to King Haakon?'

The clerk's eyes are round. *The King?* he mouths to the manager, who is similarly agog. He's already imagining the delight of informing his other guests, the reflected glory of having a celebrity in their midst.

The young clerk has other plans. It's not long before he's on the telephone, announcing to all the local news men that Roald Amundsen, the man renowned for challenging Captain Scott to a race to the South Pole, has just checked in to Hadley's Orient Hotel. The fact that he has important telegrams to send just adds to the growing sense of intrigue that will draw every journalist for miles around to camp outside, hoping to break the news of Amundsen's polar victory. Or possibly his defeat.

As for Amundsen, telegrams and celebrity can wait. Now installed in the royal suite on the top floor of the hotel, the explorer sinks shoulder-deep in a bathtub of hot water, his longed-for desire fulfilled. Only now does he allow his mind to trace back over his journey from Bunde Fjord in Norway to the very ends of the earth. The years of meticulous planning have certainly paid off. The many favours asked, the many risks taken, the many crises averted – he can say now that it has all been worth it.

But how will history view my latest polar conquest? he wonders to himself. *Will I be remembered for my dedication, my discipline, my daring; or merely my deception?*

CHAPTER ONE

EARLY SEPTEMBER 1910 – MADEIRA

Flies gather in their thousands, a vibrating black swarm animating the air. A man might jump overboard to escape but the dogs don't mind. They rip into the chunks of flesh carved off the horse carcass, savouring the succulent meat and gnawing on bone fragments. It's the second such feast this week and a welcome respite from the usual ration of dried fish they've been getting on the four-week sea voyage from Norway.

Captain Thorvald Nilsen regards the scene with a sour expression. 'Yet more muck to clean up.'

Twice a day the decks of the *Fram* are sluiced with buckets of salt water. Necessary toil for the twenty men aboard when travelling with a cargo of ninety-seven sledge dogs. Fouling is only one issue. The fighting has been more or less constant. Not surprising given they're occupying every available space on deck. Until accustomed to living in such close quarters, the dogs will remain chained. They're a vicious lot. Already they've attacked the Madeira official who attempted a health inspection the evening of their arrival on the Portuguese island; and all of Captain Nilsen's carrier pigeons have disappeared, leaving only feathers. The captain scarcely needs a reason to deliver a swift kick to the unlucky dog that gets under his feet.

'Mind your manners,' he bellows when growled at.

The dogs have been divided up, with men assigned to each group. Among Roald Amundsen's dogs are three inseparable friends that he has christened 'the Three Musketeers'. United in their hatred of the chief, they snarl whenever he approaches. Amundsen considers it safest to deliver the horsemeat on a long stick, which he also uses to offer a back scratch. 'You'll come around,' he says soothingly. 'All in good time.'

Captain Nilsen scoffs.

Amundsen appreciates the reason for the captain's dark mood. He too is unsettled by what lies ahead. There is still much uncertainty. But the time is fast approaching when the whole affair will be resolved.

One by one Amundsen's dogs flop onto their sides, their bellies full to bursting. Not a bad spot to sleep off a feeding frenzy, in the shade of the tarpaulins that have been rigged up against the powerful sun. Here, off the coast of north Africa, the heat is cruel punishment for creatures with such an overabundance of fur. Just as well they won't be staying long in Madeira, their only port of call on the five-month sea journey to Antarctica. Of course the dogs don't know they're heading to Antarctica. Neither does the crew.

Captain Nilsen is getting tired of keeping Amundsen's secret. For months he's perpetuated the lie that the Arctic is their final destination, that they will round the bottom of South America and sail up the other side, all the way to the Bering Strait, where they'll enter the Arctic Ocean and drift in the sea ice across the North Pole. The crew, the expedition sponsors, Fridtjof Nansen (Amundsen's mentor and the owner of the ship), even the Norwegian parliament and the king and queen have been sold the same lie. But why head north now when the prize has already been seized by not one but two men – Peary and Cook both claiming to have reached the North Pole.

'You better be lucky down there at the South Pole. Because you'll be thrown into prison if you're not!

And probably me too.' Captain Nilsen finds it increasingly hard to hold his tongue when it's just the two of them.

'Luck has nothing to do with it,' is Amundsen's cool reply.

The captain knows Amundsen well enough to realise he will achieve his aim; but he won't make any friends in the process. Least of all Captain Scott, the English polar explorer who has made clear his intention to be the first person to reach the southernmost point on the globe. He's already on his way.

Several of the crewmen are suspicious by now. The more experienced ones have voiced the opinion that it would be madness to erect a hut on the Arctic sea ice, yet the hut they built in Amundsen's garden and then took apart was loaded into the ship's hold. Still others have questioned the logic of bringing sledge dogs all the way from Norway, when they'll supposedly be passing Alaska, home of the finest huskies.

'Now that we're in Madeira,' Nilsen's tone softens, 'do you think it might be time to let the cat out of the bag?'

Amundsen smiles. 'Well of course. That was always the plan. Get to Madeira, figure out who wants to join us. Whoever doesn't can return to Norway with my brother.'

Leon. Captain Nilsen does not envy that hapless man. He'll be the one to notify Fridtjof Nansen that Amundsen has absconded with the *Fram* – Nansen's precious vessel, the first ship purpose-built for polar research. Leon will also have to tell the king about Roald Amundsen's radical change of plan. He alone will shoulder the burden. They'll be long gone by then. Not even a king's decree will reach the *Fram* once it leaves Madeira.

CHAPTER TWO

'This one's pregnant.' Oscar Wisting runs a hand over the dog's belly.

'Just what we need, more disgusting dogs cluttering up my deck,' mutters the captain.

Oscar jerks his head in surprise. 'What? Don't you like them?' He's already formed a deep attachment to his ten dogs. Camilla is one of his favourites. And now he has an excuse to increase her rations. They greet their master with howls of uncontained joy, especially on the days when Oscar mixes the dried fish with a generous dollop of beef fat and boiled cornmeal. The more intelligent dogs have worked out that this treat is dished up every third day. Others just apply their intelligence to stealing from neighbours.

The night is warm. The crew gathers on deck. They've been told an important announcement is coming. Hjalmar Johansen squeezes in beside Helmer Hansen. Both men are seasoned Arctic adventurers. Both have their suspicions that all is not what it seems aboard the *Fram*.

'What do you think?' says Johansen knowingly. 'Are we finally going to find out what's going on?'

The two men chuckle. They've shared their theories with a few others aboard and there's a certain nervous tension in the air. Amundsen appears before the assembled men. He's an imposing figure, tall, with a regal bearing. The serious set of his face, his unwavering gaze and his large hooked nose lend a heroic cast to his appearance. He is, after all, a world-famous explorer, the first man to navigate the Northwest Passage. The one man who succeeded where so many had died trying. They're all a bit awed by his reputation. All except Johansen, that is. He has his own impressive reputation.

Amundsen's brother Leon, who has been heavily involved in expedition planning, stands to one side with Captain Nilsen, who flicks the edge of a rolled-up chart back and forth with his fingernail in an obsessive fashion. Leon's eyes dart from man to man. Roald stands erect, his expression unreadable.

Finally the great explorer speaks. 'Thank you for waiting so patiently, and thank you for your hard work. Our first weeks together have been most enjoyable. As you're aware, I've chosen each of you for your strong character. Ours is an ambitious expedition and I require a certain type of individual, capable of adapting to changing conditions. You each have much to contribute and I trust we will end our association not only as colleagues but as friends. I have no doubt that you will be tested greatly in the coming months, but I have perhaps one of the greatest tests for you tonight.' Amundsen pauses and asks the captain to unroll his chart.

And there it is. Antarctica. Johansen chortles to himself. He finally understands the need for secrecy, and the absurd excuses for all the odd preparations.

'I have deceived you,' says Amundsen flatly. 'We will not be heading round the Horn and up through the Bering Strait towards the North Pole. We are in fact heading due south. To Antarctica. To the South Pole.'

Amundsen examines the men's faces. This is shattering news and they're clearly dumbfounded. Except Johansen, of course, who has a grin spreading from ear to ear. Johansen elbows Helmer in the ribs. He too starts to smile. They're going to race Captain Scott to the South Pole. No wonder Amundsen had to keep his true intentions a secret.

'Anyone who wishes to be released from his contract must leave the *Fram* by tomorrow morning and return to Norway with my brother Leon. I will cover all the costs of your return travel.'

The smiles prove contagious. Each man turns to his neighbour and starts to talk. Several crewmen draw closer to Nilsen's chart and point at the big black dot at the centre of the continent, drawing a line with their fingers out to the coast.

Captain Nilsen's voice rises above the hubbub. 'We need you each to signal your commitment to the new plan.'

Amundsen is already circulating among the men. He's noticed Johansen, read his enthusiastic expression. 'Up for adventure, Johansen?'

'Never been readier.'

Amundsen nods mildly at the man Fridtjof Nansen insisted he bring on the expedition, practically made it impossible to refuse. The fact still irks him.

Adolf Lindstrøm doesn't wait to be asked. 'You'll need a cook,' he says, clasping Amundsen's shoulders and planting a kiss on each cheek.

The familiarity doesn't bother the chief – not from Lindstrøm, his beloved Northwest Passage cook. 'Good on you, Fatty,' he says.

'And you, Helmer?' Another veteran of the Northwest journey, Helmer is a restless spirit with unstinting loyalty. Amundsen barely needs to ask. Oscar Wisting is swept along by the excitement. He's suddenly laughing with the national ski champion, Olav Bjaaland, at the boldness of the plan, at what's being asked of them. Both lack experience and yet both are quick to offer their support.

Jørgen Stubberud squeezes in to shake Amundsen's hand with his strong carpenter's grip. 'You've got me hook, line and sinker, sir.'

Relief eases the knot in Amundsen's chest as more men pledge themselves to the expedition. For a whole year he's held his secret so close. Now, with so many hands to shake, so many agreeing to accompany him, Amundsen allows the tension to leave his body. Who would have thought that revealing his hand would be so freeing?

'Looks like you'll be going home on your own,' Amundsen says to his brother. 'I'll get the men to write to their families – tell them of the change in plan. You can take the letters with you.' He reaches into his pocket and retrieves two envelopes. 'Two from me to deliver. One to Nansen. One to the king.'

Leon swallows hard.

Amundsen ignores the feeble gesture and proffers a slip of paper. 'You'll need to send a telegram too.'

Leon looks down. The wording is simple and direct:

Captain Scott Terra Nova Christchurch

Beg inform you Fram proceeding Antarctica. Amundsen.

'This is it, Leon,' says Amundsen with obvious delight. 'Whether Scott likes it or not. The race is on.'

December 1887 – Bunde Fjord, Norway

The fifteen-year-old shivers as he wedges his bedroom window open with a rag. Even if the wind picks up, it won't slam shut. He hopes it will snow in the night, forcing the temperature in his bedroom well below zero. The colder the better. Suffering is part of the pleasure. Tucked under his bedclothes, Roald waits until his breath turns white. Only then does he reach for his book.

Sir John Franklin's men are starved. On the Coppermine River there is no game to hunt. They've covered a thousand kilometres and mapped a small section of the Arctic coast. Fort Enterprise lies a week's march away, but they are exhausted. They have nothing to eat. They make do with foraged lichen and boil up the leather from their spare boots. Two men find a maggot-ridden carcass abandoned by a pack of wolves. It's a hearty meal for dying men.

'What are you doing?' Roald's mother exclaims, bustling into the room. 'You'll catch your death of cold.'

'Leave it open, I like the fresh air,' Roald says from behind the cover of Journey to the Shores of the Polar Sea.

'Nonsense.' Roald's mother wrenches the rag free and snaps the window shut. 'I've just lost your father. I don't want to lose a son.'

Roald does not need reminding that his father is dead and his older brothers have all left home. 'Leave me please, Mother,' he says with tenderness. 'I'm enjoying my book.'

'Sir John Franklin,' Roald's mother muses, tilting the cover of the book. 'Is that the Arctic explorer?'

'The very same,' says Roald distractedly, his gaze once again glued to the text.

'Don't you get any ideas now,' she says, heading for the door. 'You're going to go to medical school.'

Roald doesn't want to be a doctor; he would rather become an Arctic explorer and be hungry, frozen and close to death. Roald slips out of bed and once again wedges his window open.

CHAPTER THREE

'So where have these books been hiding?' asks Johansen, his
tone implying slyness on the part of the chief.

'Hiding in plain view.' Amundsen's reply is curt.
'They've been on the bookshelf since we left Norway. You
just didn't notice them.'

Johansen picks up a copy of *The Voyage of the Discovery*,
Captain Scott's account of his first journey to Antarctica
and his attempt to push as far south as possible. Judging by
its dog-eared appearance it's been pored over. Other books
are scattered across the dining table. All great men, these
pioneers of Antarctic exploration – James Clarke Ross,

Borchgrevink, Armitage, Ernest Shackleton, and of course Robert Falcon Scott. Johansen gives a half laugh. He's written his own book. *With Nansen in the North* was the title. A written account of an epic journey. Maybe not a classic of polar literature. But who knows, maybe he'll chronicle his Antarctic adventures and call it: *With Amundsen in the South*.

Since learning of their true destination, the men have behaved like schoolboys, joking, singing and debating their prospects of being first at the southernmost point of the globe. Unlike schoolboys, they're motivated to do their homework. They all feel ill-equipped.

Settled into the corner of the wardroom, Helmer has his nose in the first volume of *The Heart of the Antarctic*, which chronicles Shackleton's journey to 88 degrees south – so far, the world record. Clothing, travel and food, dog driving and survival in conditions of almost unbearable severity – there's not much Helmer doesn't know after spending so many years exploring the Arctic. He's always hungry for adventure, but he's troubled by how little he knows about the great white continent.

'You'll have to hurry through that Shackleton,' says Stubberud to Helmer. 'No point me starting the story at Volume Two.'

'Easy now, big boy. We've got months yet,' Helmer scoffs.

'Well, I'll need months. I'm not much of a reader,' says Stubberud. 'I prefer to smoke my pipe of an evening.'

There's one book on the table that should be of particular interest. *Belgica Diary: The First Scientific Expedition to the Antarctic*. Nobody has noticed but the name of the author is stamped on the spine as plain as day – Roald Amundsen.

Amundsen picks up the book he wrote almost fifteen years ago. Serving as first mate on a Belgian expedition to Antarctica was his big break, working without pay to get his foot in the door. Securing a place on any kind of polar expedition was nearly impossible without experience. As a lad he'd ventured out on his own in and around Norway, but claiming to be well-organised, a strong skier and an able seaman counted for little. To be taken seriously he'd had to climb up from the bottom and prove himself in many surprising ways. Working amid the appalling filth and butchery of the Norwegian sealing fleet had little to recommend it, but in so doing Amundsen had obtained the necessary qualifications to command his own boat. That had been his ticket to Antarctica, and while the *Belgica* expedition was hellish in all respects, it did mark the beginning of an illustrious career. Amundsen closes the book. Some of the memories are still painful. He's invested much in his Antarctic ambitions. Now it's time to bring it all to bear.

Up on deck Captain Nilsen stands firm at the wheel and glances intermittently at the sails. Nilsen follows the old Portuguese shipping route that will initially take them out across the Atlantic Ocean and towards Brazil. From there, they'll meet the south-east trade winds which will whip them back towards South Africa where their journey will tend ever southward. Human civilisation dissolves into the eastern horizon. The dogs indulge in a chorus of celebratory howling.

'We're nothing but a floating kennel,' sighs Nilsen as he scans the sky. He's got other concerns – sailing the *Fram* all the way to Antarctica with two sails instead of four on the foremast and two where there could be three on the jib-boom. He'd love a full set, but the budget wouldn't stretch. He checks the hour. Time for Sverre Hassel to take over the next watch. The captain looks forward to being relieved of his duties by the dog handler. He stretches his neck first one way then the other, waiting for the reassuring click as he watches Sverre argue his way along the deck with tender-hearted Oscar cradling something in his jacket.

'What's the fuss, you two?'

Oscar looks annoyed. 'My dog, Camilla, she had her puppies – four of them. Last night.'

'And?' The captain yawns.

'A couple of other dogs got hold of them. Ate three. Only this one left.' Oscar peers into his jacket.

'Nature's a cruel mistress . . .' The captain feels no pity. His own pigeons met a similar fate.

'Sverre wants to toss it overboard,' Wisting says suddenly. 'Because it's female.'

Captain Nilsen gives a shrug.

Oscar draws his jacket in tighter. 'How can you do that to an innocent creature?'

'We've got more than enough bitches,' Sverre says. 'It's a shame it was the three male pups that were eaten. I would have liked to keep them.'

'Don't go arguing with our resident dog expert.' The captain offers Sverre the wheel.

'More like resident monster. Just look . . .' Oscar opens his jacket to reveal the tiny bundle. 'Imagine throwing this beautiful creature overboard.'

The captain's gaze is temporarily waylaid by the tiny silken puppy. He finds himself reaching out to touch its impossibly soft fur. A murmur escapes. Not from the pup but from the captain. 'The others eaten, really?'

Sverre gives a sniff of indifference. 'Happens all the time. And I can guarantee you it is a hundred times more traumatic for the pup and the poor mother than a swift drowning.'

'Give him here,' Nilsen says suddenly.

Oscar looks unsure. 'You're not going to chuck her over the side, are you?'

'Course not – I'm no monster!'

Oscar hands the pup over. It roots under the captain's arm, its pinkish nose seeking a mother. The captain coos.

Sverre and Oscar swap amused looks. With his bellowing dislike of the dogs, the captain is the least likely of anyone to be taken in by their cuteness. But he has obviously fallen suddenly and deeply in love. 'You've got it wrong, Sverre,' he says airily. 'This dog is a male.'

Sverre snorts. As if the captain would know. He hasn't even looked at the business end!

'He can doss down in my cabin. He'll be safe with me. Won't you boy? You'll be safe with Cappy.' Without another word, Nilsen heads away with the pup sheltering in his upturned shirt. A few of the dogs lunge at him as he passes.

'Back off, puppy killers!' Nilsen taunts.

In the charthouse Martin Rønne sits at his Singer sewing machine just as he does all day every day, turning out endless orders for his shipmates – repairs, duffle bags, clothing, shoes, leatherwork.

'Do you have any offcuts? Something for a little bed?'

Rønne stops sewing and looks up.

'My new friend.' Nilsen gestures at the puppy in his arms.

Rønne's eyes widen.

'He's called Madeiro,' Nilsen says proudly.

'I didn't think you liked dogs.' Rønne hands the captain a length of canvas.

The captain gives a fulsome laugh. 'I do like this fellow. I snatched him from the jaws of death. His three brothers got eaten alive.'

'Doesn't surprise me,' Rønne grunts, pumping the treadle to get the sewing machine back up to speed. 'Give them half a chance, those beasts would eat a man.'

CHAPTER FOUR

Back in Norway, Fridtjof Nansen is annoyed. It's servants' work, tending fires. But having allowed the fire in the grate to burn itself out, he is once again cold. 'Do not disturb me,' he had told them, 'I have important work.' *And now look at the important work I am to do*, he thinks, kneeling in front of the fireplace and blowing the cinders until they redden.

Nansen grasps the corner of his desk and heaves himself to his feet. He's thought of a title at least – for the history of early Arctic exploration he's been writing. It will be two volumes by the time he's shared everything he has to say on the topic. Again the thought occurs to him that it's the closest he'll come to polar adventures now that he's past the age of playing an active role. Lucky Johansen, to be back in the fray. His trusted polar companion is heading to the ice. A chance at redemption. He's got himself into a sorry state in recent years. Hopefully he can swap his personal troubles for another adventure. Nansen sighs at the prospect of an old age spent in committee rooms, listening, talking, but never *doing*.

The housekeeper appears at the door. 'Sorry sir. I know you asked not to be disturbed, but there's a visitor. Says it's urgent. Mr Amundsen.'

'Good grief! Is it his ghost?'

'He looks real enough to me,' the housekeeper says. 'Shall I show him in?'

'By all means!' Nansen swings his chair expectantly to the door as the housekeeper disappears. He prays that nothing has happened to his ship. Lending Amundsen the *Fram* was a symbolic gesture. Time to hand him the reins. Was it too soon? What could possibly have happened? The door to the hall creaks open again.

'Here's Mr Amundsen,' the housekeeper says as she hurries over to the dying fire.

Nansen raises his eyebrows in sudden comprehension. 'Ah, the *other* Mr Amundsen.'

The visitor extends his hand. It is clammy, unpleasant to the touch. Nansen draws his hand away and sits down, wiping his palm on the arm of the chair as he pulls it closer to his desk. 'Any news of your brother?'

Leon clears his throat. 'Actually I have quite a lot to report.'

Nansen peers around at the housekeeper, assessing her progress with the fire. His tone is tentative. 'All well?'

'Fine. I've just got back from Madeira. The *Fram* set sail from there three weeks ago. I've got a letter for you. One also for the king.'

Nansen's cheeks are flushed as he accepts the envelope and fumbles his glasses on. 'Let's see. Important news for me *and* the King of Norway. Well, well, let's see now . . .'

Three swift strokes and it's open. Nansen's eyes slide over the handwritten page, his expression growing increasingly stern.

Dear Professor Nansen

It has not been easy to write you these lines, but there is no way to avoid it, and therefore I will just have to tell you straight . . .

Amundsen has left nothing out – his crushing disappointment when the North Pole was conquered and his own dreams of securing that prize were shattered; his desire to accomplish something truly worthwhile with all the preparations he had already made towards achieving that victory; his decision to strike out for the South Pole and the need for absolute secrecy to avoid giving Captain Scott the upper hand. Acutely aware of the friendship that exists between Nansen and Captain Scott and the close ties his mentor has with Great Britain, Amundsen is keen to demonstrate his remorse.

There have been many times I have almost confided this secret to you, but then turned away, afraid that you would stop me. I have often wished that Scott could have known my decision, so that it did not look like I tried to get ahead of him without his knowledge. But I have been afraid that any public announcement would stop me . . .

I am currently sending the king the same message, but nobody else. A couple of days after you receive this message, my brother (Leon Amundsen) will make a public announcement.

Once more I beg you. Do not judge me too harshly. I am no hypocrite, but rather was forced by distress to make this decision. And so, I ask you to forgive me for what I have done. May my future work make amends for it.

Respectfully yours,
Roald Amundsen

Nansen shakes his head wearily and gets to his feet. There's a shriek as Nansen's chair tips backwards onto the housekeeper tending the fire. He doesn't seem to notice and he fails to apologise to the poor woman. He inhales deeply. 'That idiot.'

Embarrassed and a little scared, Leon draws his head in like a turtle.

With a sudden show of rage, Nansen grasps Roald's letter in his fist and cries, 'Why didn't he tell me he was going to race Scott to the South Pole?'

For some time Leon has imagined Nansen's fury at Roald's bald-faced lies. Now all he wants is to shrink from view. Leon starts to apologise but Nansen cuts him off.

'That bloody fool! If only I had known about his plan, I could have helped him!'

CHAPTER FIVE

No more soups. No more washing in fresh water. Captain's orders.

'We'll just have to bathe in rum,' somebody shouts.

Amundsen's hand silences the laughter. 'Soap will lather just as well in salt water.'

'What about the water stored in the longboat, sir? Do we have to drink that?'

'We'll keep that for the dogs.'

There's a collective sigh of relief. The water crisis is not yet so bad that they have to drink the rusty water that has turned the dog turds bright red. But it may yet get worse if nature doesn't deliver. The great downpours, usually so predictable in these latitudes, have failed to show. If it doesn't rain soon, they'll have to go ashore in the Americas. A waste of precious time as far as Amundsen is concerned. Progress has already been delayed. The north-east trade winds died out earlier than expected. The stiff breeze that so eased their transit across the Atlantic has now shifted south, making their approach to the equator a true battle of man versus the elements. If the doldrums had lived up to their reputation, the *Fram* could have quite happily motored across the calm waters, her engines taking up the slack in the sails. As it stands, the final degrees of latitude to the equator have been hard won against a brutal southerly.

'What about crossing the line?' asks the carpenter Stubberud. 'Can we still do that?'

Amundsen invites Nilsen to speak. As captain of the ship, all seafaring traditions are his responsibility. A number of men aboard have not crossed the equator before. Depending on one's point of view, King Neptune's initiation ritual can be a laugh or an ordeal.

Nilsen shakes his head. 'It's not the water situation. Not enough room on deck, lads.'

There's grumbling. Mostly from those men who have already undergone the humiliation of being covered in paint, performing in a beauty contest or forced to eat foul substances. It should be their turn to inflict suffering on others.

Stubberud is up for any activity that relieves the boredom of months at sea. He shouts, 'I was hoping to be tarred and feathered, sir!'

'The pigeons haven't left us much in the way of feathers. How about we cover you in dog—'

'Men!' Amundsen calls for quiet. Keeping up morale is important; they still have so far to travel. 'How about a celebratory dinner instead with music, some cigars and liqueurs.'

It is symbolic for Amundsen too, this tipping over the imaginary line from the Northern to the Southern Hemisphere. Has he got away with it? Is Nansen furious? Has he offended the king? Does the Norwegian parliament demand an explanation? Or worse, demand the money they lent the expedition? Now that they are underway, nothing else matters. To assign any importance to these questions is pointless.

Suddenly there's a loud clattering noise, a yowling from below. One of the dogs has fallen down the stairs. Oscar scrambles down and brings the poor whimpering creature back up on deck. He calls to Sverre.

The dog expert sees immediately. 'Broken his leg.'

'How did he break free?' asks the captain.

Sverre lifts the ragged rope dangling from the dog's collar. 'Gnawed his way free. Should be called Houdini.'

'It's my Isak,' says Oscar of the massive creature. 'I'd know him anywhere. Must have landed with his full weight on that leg. I suppose you'll want to throw him overboard now,' Oscar says with cynicism, convinced that this animal will be another casualty of the expedition's hard line on population control.

Lieutenant Gjertson speaks up. 'I can set the bone.'

As if sensing salvation, the dog starts to wag its tail, proud of its double achievement – escaping both captivity and walking the plank.

'We need to let the children loose,' says Amundsen to the captain. 'It's been more than six weeks. Their paws are swollen. Their claws are falling off.'

Captain Nilsen looks doubtful. Puppy killers spring to mind. 'There'll be bloodshed.'

'Entertainment for the men,' Amundsen says playfully. Unlike Nilsen he trusts the dogs. Most are quite tame now, used to their human handlers and the routine of life at sea. Even the Three Musketeers allow a scratch behind the ears.

'Not my idea of fun,' says Nilsen. 'I like having a full set of limbs.'

Men being mauled isn't Amundsen's concern. The problem is with dogs attacking each other. It's the only fun they know; they've been deprived of the pleasure for months. But there's one way to avoid all-out carnage.

Amundsen calls to Sverre, 'Got those dog muzzles somewhere accessible?'

The next morning everybody is on deck to witness the great untying of the dogs – it's the closest thing to sport in the mid-Atlantic. Even the men who should be sleeping off night watch prefer to witness the spectacle. Sverre demonstrates how the men should fit the muzzles, allowing for jaw movement but not the use of teeth. Captain Nilsen retreats below deck. So does Rønne, complaining loudly about all the work he has piling up at his sewing machine. Neither man wants to be on the battlefield.

At first nothing happens. The dogs seem perfectly happy to remain on their home patch. The *Fram*'s bow cleaves through the waves and every now and then a shower of sea spray casts a wide net over the animals. Under the circumstances, the dogs prefer to hunker down than venture forth. Only one dog lifts its nose to the southerly wind and gives a sniff. Amazingly, it's Isak, the fresh splint on his leg, the only dog to have earned his freedom. Curious perhaps to follow a smell on the ocean breeze, Isak hobbles on three good legs along the rising-and-falling deck among dogs that, despite being at sea together, have remained complete strangers throughout the voyage, thanks to being tied at opposite ends of the ship. There are growls, then a surge, sudden and savage. At least a dozen dogs bring the curious interloper down. Shrieks, wailing and whimpers surround the hash of animals setting to with furious excitement. Other dogs leap to their feet, surprised by their lack of restraints. Other fights break out. Aghast, the men look on, horrified at the carnage they've unleashed. Nobody intervenes. To do so would be suicide . . . or perhaps not.

Amundsen roars with laughter. 'Perfect!' he calls to Sverre. 'Plenty of fur flying but no blood.' It's just what the dogs needed, a good scrap. And the men. It looks like everyone's enjoying the sudden change in the shipboard dynamic.

Helmer rocks back and forth with amusement. 'I love being back with Amundsen,' he shouts to nobody in particular. It's the ocean, heading for the ice, the howling of the wind and the howling of the dogs – all of it music to his ears. 'This is where I belong – it's like the Northwest Passage all over again!'

Sverre smiles and nods. His Arctic experiences were with another Norwegian explorer, Otto Sverdrup. He recognises blind loyalty; it's unmistakable. Helmer would dive to the bottom of the ocean if Amundsen asked. The chief has chosen his team wisely, Sverre concedes. Then again, not everyone aboard is as loyal as Helmer.

CHAPTER SIX

Johansen has a serious set to his face as he works. The calm of the little workshop Bjaaland has set up below decks suits him. Bjaaland is grateful for the help. Adjusting twenty pairs of hickory skis to suit each member of the crew is a fiddly task, made trickier by rough seas tossing equipment every which way. For a time the two men talk about Captain Scott. Nobody ever seems to tire of discussing the British reaction to Amundsen's plan or the fury they must feel at being unwittingly drawn into a race. Inevitably the conversation turns to their own expectations of success and the various advantages they hope will secure a Norwegian victory.

'Amundsen did well, getting a man of your calibre to join this escapade,' says Bjaaland.

Johansen shrugs. 'Could say the same of you: Norway's champion skier!'

Bjaaland can't help smiling. 'You know it's funny, wherever I am, whatever I'm doing, I'd rather be someplace else. I met Amundsen in a train station in Germany. I was travelling with the Norwegian ski team to a competition in France. I told him I'd like to ski to the North Pole. He offered to take me with him.'

'You're his ticket to a swift victory. That's what Amundsen wants – speed. To snatch the prize from Scott.' Johansen takes off his cap and runs a hand over his close-cropped white hair. He's slightly older than the rest, or at least he seems to be. The whole nation knows of his adventures with Nansen in the Arctic. He may be only forty-three years old, but Johansen's already lived a thousand lives.

'I read your book,' says Bjaaland, proud to finally have a chance to mention it. Still, he is self-conscious enough around the renowned adventurer to avoid eye contact.

'Did you like it?'

'I did. Must have been incredible. Being with Nansen.'

Johansen hums agreement.

'So what's he like?'

'Nansen?' Johansen rubs his chin. 'The best. He saved my life.'

'I thought you saved his life.'

'I did.'

The two men laugh then retreat into companionable silence.

After a minute Bjaaland asks, 'So what happened?' He's like a child eager for a retelling of a favourite tale.

'A polar bear struck me on the head. I would have been mincemeat. That big boy was twice the size of a man. Nansen shot him. And then we ate him. I think Nansen probably couldn't bear the thought of being left alone so far from civilisation.' Johansen grins.

'Good thing there are no polar bears where we're going,' Bjaaland says.

'Plenty of crevasses that'll swallow you whole.'

Bjaaland selects a fresh pair of skis and runs his hand admiringly down their length. 'Extra long skis are a good idea. Hard to disappear down a crack with these on your feet.'

After a short silence, Bjaaland eases the conversation back to adventure. 'When I was reading your book, I'd never have imagined that I'd be with the man who set out with Nansen to discover the North Pole.'

'If only we'd succeeded . . .'

'That doesn't really matter. It was the furthest north anyone had ever been. Before Peary. Or Cook. Whoever reached it!'

'I'd like to know how they did it,' Johansen says. 'Hard to make any progress north, when the ice you're on is constantly drifting south.' He remembers the days of frustration all too keenly. After a full day's march, to end the day in more or less the same place. Ridiculous.

'Of course failing to wind the chronometers put us at a slight disadvantage . . .' Johansen trails off, his understatement left hanging as he recalls the feeling of dread at having no way of determining their position or that of the *Fram*. Things had progressed from bad to worse with the sea ice breaking up, leaving them to bob about on an ice floe for more than a month. All the dogs were dead by that stage. Thankfully they had the kayaks, although one had been badly mauled by a walrus. They were lucky not to be savaged themselves. What sweet relief to finally reach terra firma. Franz Josef Land. Uninhabited, unfortunately, but a safe place to make a decent shelter from walrus hide and enjoy eight months of waiting for winter to pass so they could get going again. At least they'd had plenty to eat. Walrus, polar bear – they'd exacted revenge on those two species. Johansen sighs. 'Quite a time we had.'

Johansen steps back from the work bench. For a moment he looks thoughtful. A return to the ice. This is really all he wants. Not the comfortable existence of a husband and father, warming his legs by the fire as his wife, Hilda, bustles about and children squabble. Domestic life – such a brutal disappointment when contrasted with a fight for survival. How close he and Nansen came to death; how alive he felt in its presence.

'Well, you're in for another adventure. With another great explorer.'

'You know, I get the distinct impression that Amundsen does not want me here.'

'Really?'

'Well, he hand-picked everyone else himself. I'm quite sure I'm only here because of Nansen.'

Bjaaland snorts in disbelief. 'You've got more experience than anybody. Even Amundsen.'

Johansen sucks in his breath with displeasure. 'Be careful now. Comments like that . . .'

Bjaaland blushes. 'Sorry, I just thought—'

'Hey, it's all fine!' Johansen says, shrugging off his truthfulness with a light-hearted tone. 'Me? All I care about is getting to the South Pole.'

CHAPTER SEVEN

With the Roaring Forties behind them, the Norwegians must now face the Furious Fifties and the kind of violent winds and treacherous sailing conditions that their Viking forebears would have welcomed. The west wind belt is living up to its reputation. Foul weather bears down on the *Fram* with a force that would be frightening if it wasn't pushing the ship in the right direction. Aided by the gale blowing at her heels, the *Fram* gallops the remaining distance across the Southern Atlantic, and even running short of sails, the ship is catapulted around the southern tip of Africa. There'll be no slowing now. Those wishing to admire the Cape of

Good Hope will be disappointed; they're too far south. It is mid-November. The Norwegians are more than halfway to Antarctica. From here on, theirs will be a lonely trek into one of the world's emptiest stretches of ocean.

Dwarfing the ship, the dark sea gathers off the stern, threatening to swallow it whole or at least wipe clean the deck. Already two dogs have been lost overboard. But the ship's rounded hull is well suited to riding out the immense waves that loom up in endless procession. Like a lady hoisting her petticoats to step over a muddy puddle, the *Fram* simply lifts herself up, allowing whatever monster is gathering to pass under her hull. Unfortunately the clever hull design gives rise to a vile side-to-side roll and is responsible for much retching.

Fresh water is still in short supply. They get a thorough soaking at least once a day from the north-west but the downpours don't last long. Neither does the sleet or hail that charges in on sudden gusts, lashing the decks and pummelling the poor dogs with short-lived fury. The sun reappears just as abruptly, working with a determined westerly to dry the decks and restore some comfort to the animals, who are looking thin and miserable. Regular feeds of butter are deemed the most efficient way of improving their diet. To be of any use in Antarctica, they need fattening up.

Oscar doles out gobs of yellow butter onto the deck.

'If we keep feeding the dogs like this, there'll be none left for us humans.'

'The dogs are more important than you or me.' Sverre shows his empty hands to a particularly insistent dog. 'The whole outcome of this expedition depends on them. You want to be successful or eat pancakes?'

Oscar offers Camilla a second helping of butter off his hand. She's no longer the only mother. Ester had six pups, as did Sara. Eva had seven. Kaisa, Bella, Lola, Katinka and Else also gave birth. Of the forty-six pups, thirty-four have been tossed into the sea, eight have been eaten by other dogs and one was snatched by an albatross.

Unlucky Isak has made a full recovery after breaking his leg and is just as likely to start a fight as any other able-bodied dog at feeding time. Freedom is no longer the novelty it once was. A clear hierarchy has been established among the dogs but every now and then hell breaks loose. Often it's over a wayward tail. Even a rogue wave can start a brawl. In the dogs' world, it seems that neighbours must take the blame for the sheer awfulness of shipboard life: the cold, the frightful wind, the constant hateful wetness. Sea water has made them footsore. Many shed great flakes of skin and clumps of fur. The smart dogs slink below deck in search of dry lodgings. Any luxury is short-lived. Recently the chief stoker yanked Camilla from a warm spot between the pistons. If they'd fired up the engines, she'd have been crushed. Such miserable whines could be heard when she was returned to the wet deck with the others; meanwhile her puppy lies warm and dry in the captain's berth.

Despite his devotion to Madeiro, Nilsen's patience for the dogs is wearing thin. One dog, Jakob, has the nickname 'The Murderer', so often has he snaffled the newly born. Witnessing puppies being eaten alive sends Nilsen into a violent rage. He takes to The Murderer with a chain, applying it with such severity that he almost beats the unfortunate creature to death.

'Captain!' Sverre brings Nilsen back to his senses. He takes the bloody chain from the captain's shaking hand. Everyone knows Nilsen is under enormous stress and dangerously short on sleep. Icebergs are the reason. They may excite some aboard, but for Nilsen there is no greater horror. Easily spotted during daylight hours, the bulbous blocks of ice are much harder to see in the dark and would breach their thick hull as if it were made of butter. Such accidents have been known to sink a ship before the crew can even scramble from their berths. Keeping alert during a six-hour watch through the night requires lots of hot, strong coffee. As an added precaution, Nilsen asks that every two hours the temperature of the ocean be checked – a disagreeable task in a squall, but infinitely preferable to sinking to Davy Jones' Locker.

CHAPTER EIGHT

Who will go ashore? It's one question preying on everyone's mind. Nobody will ask Amundsen outright. To do so would seem overeager and likely count against whoever is asking. Going ashore means having a crack at the South Pole. Instant fame and wealth, assuming a career can be forged around a victorious outcome. Each man hopes; more than half will know disappointment.

One man definitely not going ashore is Captain Nilsen. The southern winter sets in fast and he'll need to shepherd the *Fram* safely out of Antarctic waters before the sea ice weds him to the continent. His duties lie northward in

Buenos Aires, where repairs can be carried out on the *Fram* and fresh provisions taken aboard. It will be a treacherous sea journey, taking on the worst conditions in the world's most dangerous ocean regions. Many have perished rounding Cape Horn with its infamous wind, enormous waves and hazardous currents. That said, money is Nilsen's major concern. There's simply none left. Once the *Fram* makes port, they'll need to get out the begging bowl.

A number of the crew intended to leave the *Fram* in San Francisco. Of course, San Francisco was never actually on Amundsen's itinerary and these men were taken on as sailors, not polar adventurers. There is little chance of them making the cut. Besides, Nilsen will need experienced sailors to make landfall in Argentina.

At 56 degrees south, their charted course is well below Australia and heading into ever wilder latitudes. This far south there is no land to interrupt the flow of westerly winds or waylay the enormous waves circling the globe. The rotating motion of the *Fram* is a firm fixture of shipboard life. The men surrender to it, rolling like marbles whichever way they're tipped. The table and chairs are lashed to the floor and table manners are a thing of the past. What was once a respectable affair is now a comedy involving grabbing, grappling and stabbing at sliding plates of food. Everyone wishes away the remaining 1500 kilometres of their painfully long voyage.

As Christmas 1910 draws near, the smell of baking fills the cabins below deck. Lindstrøm has plenty of visitors in the galley, and a few cheeky enough to pilfer a tasty treat whenever he turns his back. Lindstrøm decides to lock up the cakes lest there be no finale to the Christmas feast he's planning.

Cakes are only one element of their celebration. On Christmas Eve Rønne hangs the great lines of colourful flags that he's made on his sewing machine. Captain Nilsen has helped decorate the wardroom and hung coloured lanterns in the passageways between the cabins. With Madeiro getting under his feet constantly and tangling himself in long strings of bunting, it's taken longer than planned. Nilsen can be heard by turns scolding the dog for getting in the way and begging for forgiveness when he steps on his paws. The fore-cabin has been thoroughly cleaned up. Helmer polishes the brass until it gleams and tries not to think of his little boy celebrating Christmas without him. His wife is no doubt used to his absences on such occasions. They had three Christmases apart last time he set sail with Amundsen. Helmer can imagine her rolling her eyes and making some comment about Amundsen being her husband's one true love.

The gramophone has been rigged up to play from Amundsen's cabin. With nineteen members of the crew making merry, there'll be little room to manoeuvre. They'd like to have organised a little concert like they had after crossing the equator, but the piano is hopelessly out of tune after months of thumping up and down on the waves.

When evening draws near, the men start to gather in the *Fram*'s fore-cabin, dressed in the best clothes they have to hand. Gone are the unkempt whiskers. The smooth faces render many of the crew scarcely recognisable. Only one unfortunate soul will remain on his own throughout the evening.

Stubberud is angry. It's his turn to take the 8 p.m. to 2 a.m. watch while everyone is eating, drinking, smoking and singing. 'I'm a carpenter, not a sailor,' he thinks aloud as he listens to the yahooing and cheering from below. He roars his displeasure at the night sky. A few of the dogs around him take up the challenge and give voice to their own complaints in yowling, wavering tones.

'That's right,' Stubberud mutters more to himself than the dogs. 'Lonely losers, all of us.'

He smells tobacco smoke before he sees Johansen. 'Sounds like some party down there.' Stubberud's words come out a little sourly.

'I've come to relieve you, brother,' Johansen says, pulling his wool cap down over his head. Gone is the chin strap beard. Johansen has shaved it off.

'Good grief!' Stubberud blurts out without fully

taking in Johansen's words. 'I didn't recognise you. What have you done to yourself?'

Johansen turns his face first one way then the other. 'What do you think?'

'More modern perhaps,' says Stubberud, thinking what a vast improvement it is.

'Felt like a change.' Johansen rubs the soft skin, the small nicks around his jawline where the razor took to its job a little too keenly. 'Last chance to see what I really look like.'

'Aye, we'll all be sprouting beards,' Stubberud agrees. He's pretty confident of being selected for the shore crew. With his experience as a carpenter, it would be absurd to remain with the ship. Of course, Johansen is guaranteed a place – after all, he's Nansen's man.

'I've come to take over the watch, Stubberud.'

'But it's not 2 a.m. yet.'

'Grub's still out. Leave it much later and you'll find crumbs. And drunken sailors snoring on the table.'

Music emanates from below, shouts, laughter.

'Come on, the offer's genuine.' Johansen nudges the carpenter away from the wheel.

Stubberud lingers a moment, not wanting to simply drop and run. 'You sure?'

'Get going before I change my mind.'

Stubberud slides down the companionway ladder towards the comforting smells and the rowdy sounds.

Everything looks festive. There's even a Christmas tree aglow with candles. A cheer goes up. Not for Stubberud but for Lieutenant Prestrud, who demonstrates that navigating is not his only skill. The satirical poem he's written for the occasion spares nobody – not even the chief – and while his performance leaves a few red faces around the table, his humour is well-intended. Amundsen raises a toast to the lieutenant.

'Good God!' Nilsen gasps when he sees Stubberud raising a glass. 'Who's at the wheel?'

Stubberud tries to calm the captain. 'It's fine. Johansen's up there.'

Nilsen sinks back into his seat. He takes a hearty swig to recover from the shock. A raucous singalong starts up in the corner. Lindstrøm carries in the tray of Christmas cakes. More shouts and whistles. Bjaaland makes space at the table for Stubberud and tops up his glass with aquavit. 'So Johansen saved the day, did he?'

'Trying to avoid temptation, I'd say.'

'What do you mean?'

Stubberud cocks an eye at his glass. 'Haven't you heard? The man's a raging alcoholic.'

CHAPTER NINE

The first icebergs appear like sentries guarding the approach to Antarctic waters. The *Fram*'s eastward journey around the globe is over. Due south is where they must point the bow now. Obligingly, the wind turns. A stiff northerly breeze fills the sails. Nothing could be better. Not good luck but good planning, Amundsen is keen to point out. Having studied every written account of vessels bound for Antarctica, he believes the best route south extends along the 175th meridian east, cutting a path as quickly as possible through the permanent belt of sea ice into the Ross Sea, which offers open waters during summer. Some vessels have languished for six weeks or more at this point in the crossing, held in the ice's clenched fists. Amundsen is adamant: no such delay for him.

The sun's rising, having never really set properly all night. He could go back to bed, but he doesn't. He's too excited. For most of the day the chief trains his binoculars on the southern horizon, in search of the telltale white line. How pleasant it will be to be surrounded by white, the ice deadening the ocean swell. They're due for a change of scene. The months at sea and the relentless daily routine aboard have started to wear thin. While one would never hope for drama, any ocean journey without incident is an exercise in monotony. Tedium can be more damaging to morale than tragedy.

It's another twenty-four hours before the cry goes out. Anybody not already on deck scrambles up the companionway to see the great white obstacle – the starting line. At first the *Fram* breaks easily through the loose sheets of ice. Wide spaces open before them like elegant avenues, allowing the boat to delve ever deeper into the white expanse. Eroded icebergs punctuate the horizon but there's nothing large enough or close enough to cause concern. Amundsen knows the *Fram* is capable of much. She may have tortured all those aboard with her unpleasant roll while crossing the Southern Ocean, but her incredible strength, rounded shape and slick surface will be more than a match for the extreme pressure of the ice squeezing her hull. Instead of being wedged in place, she'll more likely pop out of the ice like a shiny rubber ball.

'Hot soup again,' says Lindstrøm with a grin. The cook is overjoyed that the abundant supply of ice has solved the fresh water shortage. Ice means wildlife too. Fresh meat for the men. Fresh meat for the dogs to fall upon. The dogs sense movement, suddenly so much more awake to their surroundings. Amundsen dispatches Helmer and Bjaaland in a rowing boat across a stretch of water to where a group of seals bask on an ice floe. Both men are a little nervous as they approach one of the creatures. At least three metres long, it's clearly a bull. It's a matter of speculation how it will react – lollop towards the safety of the water or turn and attack the little boat and the two men? They've only got the one rifle between them. Bjaaland grips his oars, calculating how quickly he'll need to deploy them as weapons against half a tonne of blubber.

'Why isn't he making a break for it?' he asks as their boat eases closer.

'If you'd never seen a human before, would you be afraid of us?'

'One as ugly as you I would!' Bjaaland laughs uneasily. Unlike Helmer, he has no experience with such formidable beasts.

'Poor daft creature.' Helmer aims his rifle. Death is instant.

Amundsen slaps his hands on the railing. 'Helmer's a great shot,' he says to the other spectators on deck. 'Hard to drop one of those big males with a single bullet.'

The other seals on the floe seem utterly unconcerned. Only when Helmer starts to slice into the two-inch thick blubber around the animal's neck do the others bother to look up from where they are sunning themselves. Bjaaland's stomach heaves at the sight of the flensing, the steaming pile of entrails that Helmer scoops from the seal's stomach cavity with bare hands.

Watching the proceedings from the *Fram*, Lindstrøm rubs his hands together. Fresh dark meat, so rich in flavour. A mouthful of iron. Years spent in the Arctic with Amundsen have turned Lindstrøm into a master of seal meat cookery. 'Crocodile beef, we used to call it when we were in the Arctic,' he says as if reminding himself of long-lost culinary knowledge. 'You should always under- rather than overcook it.'

Oscar nods but he's not listening. Utterly absorbed by how red the blood appears against the snow, he'd love to turn away but he can't. Such purity stained with violence.

At his side Lindstrøm prattles on in his happy monologue.

A word jolts Oscar from his trance. 'Scurvy?'

'Yes, that's what I said. Fresh meat. Best cure. When we were navigating the Northwest Passage, we had no fresh provisions for three whole years. But we had seal meat. The Netsilik eat it raw. In strips. With their fingers. The women scoop up the blood in their hands and drink it straight from the animal.'

Oscar looks at the cook with horror. 'That's disgusting.'

'It's not for us to judge,' says Lindstrøm plainly. His manner is so disarming – almost childlike – and yet so often his words are the wisest spoken.

After four months of eating a mush of dried fish and cornmeal with the odd feed of butter, the Three Musketeers are initially perplexed by Amundsen's offering. They sniff warily at the blubber and entrails, give an experimental lick then set to, devouring the oddments in greedy chomps. Afterwards they can barely stand. Flopping on the deck, they succumb to sleep. From now on, the dogs will get meat every day, and not a day too soon. The sea journey has been a physical trial and many have lost condition. With this new diet so rich in fat, their scrawny frames will fill out in no time.

There are still several hundred kilometres to go before they can leave the ship but the thought of getting ashore is occupying everyone's minds. Amundsen has finally selected his party. There are more than a few men nursing wounded pride. The second mate, Lieutenant Gjertsen, is among them. Despite being desperate to continue with the expedition, the young officer's skills are needed aboard the *Fram* for the next stage of its journey. He's crestfallen to be left off the list especially as the other officer aboard, Kristian Prestrud, has made the grade. Gjertsen watches his fellow officer stuff a duffel bag with personal belongings – pairs of socks, long woollen underwear, a few books and a stiff new notebook that will no doubt record the momentous journey to the pole.

'Think of the fun you'll have in Buenos Aires,' says Prestrud, attempting to break the awkward silence. 'The food, the wine, the tango dancing.'

Gjertsen grunts. 'I'd far rather make history at the pole.'

Lindstrøm will join the shore party. Good cooking keeps spirits up and bodies in peak health. But there's also his cheerfulness, his skills as a cabinet-maker, his mechanical expertise and his famous pancakes. He'd never flaunt it, but he's one of the more seasoned polar adventurers aboard the *Fram*, having accompanied Norwegian explorer Otto Sverdrup on his map-making journey around Greenland, and travelled with Amundsen aboard the *Gjøa* on the first ever sailing of the Northwest Passage. In fact, Lindstrøm can claim the honour of being the first person to circumnavigate the Americas. Not bad for a man they all call 'Fatty'.

Jørgen Stubberud is in. The carpenter's an obvious choice. Their hut needs to survive the long polar winter.

Olav Bjaaland is also a carpenter by trade but Amundsen has chosen him for his skiing ability, hoping the national champion will pass on skills to the others. Speed is the only thing that will trump the British with their dreaded motor sledges.

'Hallelujah,' Bjaaland says. 'I'll agree to anything to get off this boat.'

Oscar Wisting is not a strong skier and has never worked a dog sledge. It's his attitude that has secured his place on Amundsen's team. He's good with his hands and can handle working in very cold conditions. Amundsen hopes he'll go well sitting behind a sewing machine. Conscientiousness is required when it comes to polar clothing and footwear – none of it must fail. It was Prestrud who recommended him for the voyage, and Amundsen has come to view him as a real asset.

Oscar's mouth drops open when he hears the news. 'I'll not let you down, sir.' His earnestness is touching. Amundsen doesn't know it yet but the mere fact of selecting Oscar for the shore party has secured the young man's undying loyalty for life.

Another man utterly devoted to Amundsen is Helmer Hansen, who has already followed Amundsen to the ends of the earth and lived to tell the tale. The Northwest Passage journey has cemented his survival skills and convinced his leader of his single-minded focus. Besides, he is one of the very few men who can meet Amundsen's steely gaze and not turn away intimidated. The chief values a man whose judgement is sound and opinions forthright.

Another plain-speaking man is the respected dog handler Sverre Hassel. He's mapped 150,000 square kilometres of Greenland by dog sledge. Nobody has a deeper understanding of the Greenland husky temperament. His expertise, his knowledge, his confidence and strong will are indispensable, particularly when it comes to the wilful and wild dogs.

Johansen will go ashore as well. To exclude him would be an affront to Nansen, and Amundsen must retain Nansen's support at all costs. Still, he's reluctant. The man is a liability. It's not just the alcoholism; Johansen has kept his drinking problem in check thus far. Rather it is the potential for conflict that has put the chief on edge. Johansen is one of Norway's most notable polar veterans and commands the men's admiration. Amundsen doesn't want him to command their loyalty too. Divided leadership is often the cause of failure of expeditions such as this. Amundsen's supreme command mustn't be called into question and yet on several occasions, Johansen has expressed his views in rather forthright tones that hint at just that. It's nothing major though. At this stage anyway.

CHAPTER TEN

Amundsen studies the newspaper article. The ink has rubbed off in the creases. The paper could fall apart in his hands, it's been folded and refolded so many times. Scott's words fade in and out of the newsprint like phantoms on the page. It's pure reflex, looking at the text, trying to get into Captain Scott's mind. He practically knows the article by heart. His rival appears so confident, this interview with a journalist a mere formality to delight his sponsors and financial backers. Amundsen shakes his head. Such valuable information given away for free! The proposed location of the English base in McMurdo Sound, the date Scott hopes to set out for the pole and the date he hopes to reach it. His means of travel, his provisions, the number of men he'll take with him – it's all there for Amundsen to judge the suitability of his own preparations against.

There's no room for Norwegians in McMurdo Sound, Amundsen has known that for a long time. The Great Ice Barrier will be their home – if they can find a safe zone. The Bay of Whales is the most likely option. Establishing their base there will place them a whole degree of latitude closer to the pole than Scott at his McMurdo base. One hundred and eleven kilometres closer. It's not much of a head start when their goal lies over a thousand kilometres to the south, but Amundsen is keen for any advantage they can muster. His biggest concern centres around Scott's plan to use motor-sledge technology. Untested as it might be, this technology could provide all the advantage Scott's camp needs to win this race.

Amundsen gets up from his desk and starts to pace back and forth. Does the Bay of Whales still exist? James Clark Ross described it in 1841. It was mentioned again by Ernest Shackleton in 1908. But the Great Ice Barrier is prone to breaking off in large chunks. Amundsen knows that. Anything could have happened in the intervening years. The Barrier rises from the sea like a perpendicular insult 50 metres high and 600 kilometres long. For two whole days the men have scowled at the uninterrupted shoreline, discussing how best to scale the great white fortifications. To land men there is one thing but to haul up all the dogs, the sledges, equipment and provisions for a year? That's another story.

Stationed atop the central mast, Bjaaland notices the broken uniformity first – a massive harbour extending as far south as the eye can see. The men on deck stare at the sudden opening in the Barrier that Amundsen promised would appear. Uncanny. Even Amundsen is surprised by the fact that the Bay of Whales appears more or less exactly as described in the written accounts.

Amundsen points emphatically. 'We need to get in there.'

'Not tonight we won't,' laughs Captain Nilsen. 'Just look at those chunks of sea ice knocking about the entrance. We'd be scuppered in an instant.'

Amundsen stalks off. To have finally arrived here and to not be able to proceed is beyond frustrating. He slams his cabin door. He wants to land, damn it! It takes a moment to calm down. *Think it through*, he tells himself. *What value lies in easy victory?*

1886 – HARDANGERVIDDA, NORWAY

Nothing grows at such altitude. At almost 2000 metres, the plateau is as empty as it is exposed; winds gust unhindered across its frozen back. Nobody dares to live there. Roald Amundsen thinks it sounds marvellous. Staring at the map he has spread across his bed, the twenty-two-year-old daydreams his challenge into being.

'Could there be anything more satisfying than being the first to cross Hardangervidda in winter?'

His brother's mind is on young women, not adventure.

'It's barely 100 kilometres wide, Leon. A two-day hike, at most. And there's a hut halfway.'

'Well . . .' Leon says.

'Skis on our feet, a reindeer sleeping bag strapped to our backs.'

Roald is very good at convincing people to do things he wants them to do. Leon's 'well' is a feeble defence, more akin to a yes than a no. And so against the advice of the locals and with little more than some chocolate, a map and a compass, the Amundsen brothers set out to conquer Hardangervidda.

When daylight fades and the wind grows more insistent and shrill, the halfway hut offers the prospect of sweet relief. But the door is nailed shut and the chimney has been boarded up to keep the snow out. In desperation Roald breaks in while Leon struggles to free up the flue. The fire they manage to light in the frozen hearth eases the pain in frozen fingers but there is nothing to eat. It is snowing heavily the next day and a second night passes. It seems much longer on empty bellies. Roald finds a sack of flour. Leon makes an unappealing slurry and heats it on the fire. He calls it porridge.

The snow continues unabated, but spurred on by their hunger, the brothers decide to press further westward, bedding down for the night in the open under big wet snowflakes that soak their clothes, destroy their map and bury their provisions.

Heavier and heavier the snowstorm swirls around the brothers on the fourth day. Without a map they stumble on: hungry, in frozen clothes, and utterly at odds with their surroundings. It's a small mercy that they've been able to drink from streams and slake their thirst. How much further? Neither can be sure. With heavy hearts they decide to turn back.

A cutting wind picks up as evening approaches. Warm wet snow has hampered their progress all day. The sodden sleeping bags are as heavy as a load of stones upon their backs. They cannot go on in the dark so seek some temporary relief behind a knoll.

'I'm digging in,' says Roald, his hands already scooping out a trench in the snow.

Lying in his hole, Roald is pleased to be out of the wind. He is cold, so desperately cold, and his body feels hollowed out from within, but sleep comes like a dark hood slipping quietly over his eyes.

By midnight he is buried alive, encased in ice so thick he cannot move a muscle to break free. Roald screams and screams but Leon does not come. Fearing for his supply of oxygen, he falls silent. What has happened? Clearly the wet snow has filled his trench and the temperature has dropped to well below freezing. Will Leon find him? Is Leon trapped also? The thought is too awful. How foolish they were to set off on such an escapade with no equipment; how naïve and stupid not to have even a tent! To suffocate in his prime with no achievements to his name – is this the price he must pay?

The bashing from above is frantic. Pounding and yelling in vain, Leon finally resorts to using a ski pole. He hacks at his brother's icy sarcophagus over several hours. He prays it is not too late. He does not want to be left alone. Not on Hardangervidda.

Roald sucks air into his lungs and frees his cramping limbs. He coughs and cries out and hugs his rescuer. Drinking in the night sky, the stars, his brother's face, he makes himself a promise to learn. Never again will he plan on the best possible outcome. It is the worst of scenarios that he needs to befriend.

CHAPTER ELEVEN

Nilsen predicted they would arrive in Antarctica on 15 January. They're a day early. If the sea ice hadn't cleared out from the Bay of Whales so swiftly, he might have hit his mark. But the captain is not a man to boast.

'Luck's on our side,' Prestrud grins.

'Some call it luck, Lieutenant,' replies Amundsen drily. 'I call it good planning.'

A few light clouds can do little against the brilliant sunshine that bounces off the calm waters of the bay. Now with a perfect landing spot offering itself up, as if on command, it does appear as though providence is smiling on the Norwegians. The Barrier surface beyond the ice foot jutting into the water is irregular but the humps and hollows and rising pressure ridges give comfort.

'See how the ice is being thrust up like that, Prestrud?' Amundsen says. 'There's got to be land underneath.' Amundsen has had a few lingering doubts as to whether it is prudent to make their base on an ever-moving ice shelf. Still, in the interests of safety they'll head inland a good few kilometres. Amundsen doesn't like the thought of their hut bobbing about on a slab of ice in the middle of the Ross Sea.

Prestrud, Helmer and Johansen set out with Amundsen on skis to check out some possible building sites. The sensation of gliding is odd after their long months at sea. Seals watch the small procession with interest as the men head across the sea ice towards the Barrier edge. There's enough fresh meat here for more than a year. The animals ignore this new threat encroaching on their colony. Ignorance is bliss. Many of them will not live out the day.

Half an hour of easy skiing gets them to the Barrier edge. But where the once-feared cliff of ice rises from the sea ice, the men find a build-up of windblown snow has created a natural ramp. Amundsen takes the gentle slope with long gliding strides. The others follow. Nothing could be easier.

Prestrud cannot help but say again, 'Extraordinary luck.'

This time Amundsen must agree. Their entry onto the Antarctic continent is utterly devoid of drama. Perhaps it is a taste of things to come.

Amundsen's looking for the perfect location for their hut. He'll know it when he sees it. The men breathe heavily, unaccustomed to such legwork after months of limited physical activity. Nobody will admit to feeling tired and nobody is cold but the ski boots are terribly uncomfortable. Too small, too stiff and with soles that are definitely too thick, the boots rub ankles and heels raw. Oscar has already spent hours unpicking the loathsome boots and trying to modify them. But it's not enough. They need more adapting. Prestrud winces with every movement of his skis. If victory is going to hurt this much, he might just swap places with Lieutenant Gjertsen after all.

Meanwhile back at the *Fram*, the seal hunt is on. The seals are at a distinct disadvantage, being scared neither of the approaching men nor of the sound of gunfire. Three seals are dispatched. A fourth figures his end is nigh and makes a break for the water, lolloping over the surface of the deep snow and sweeping up a powdery trail in his wake. Sverre takes after the frightened creature only to sink in the drift up to his thighs. He twists and heaves, breathless and unfit.

'Come back, you rotten beggar.'

The seal has no intention of doing what he asks. Sverre looks imploringly at the men watching from the *Fram* as though they might be able to offer some advice or even sympathy to the hunter.

'Don't let that seal get the better of you,' goads Stubberud. 'Show him who's boss.'

Everybody laughs. The fat Weddell seals are inquisitive to the point of foolishness and come looking for trouble. Taking pot shots from the deck isn't particularly sporting. Oscar launches breadballs at the seals to wake them up, irritating those on board who hope to score a bullseye.

'Hey! I almost had him,' complains Lieutenant Gjertsen, lowering his rifle and glowering at Oscar.

'I'm giving the poor blighter a chance.'

'A chance to be riddled with holes before I can kill him. You're a menace to man and beast.'

Captain Nilsen walks the deck and contemplates the work ahead of them. There's a lot of gear to unload and haul inland. Nilsen surveys the dogs – slumbering, mostly. They'll have to abandon their lazy habits. Hardship awaits. For his own pup too, now that he's big enough to join the fray.

Nilsen drops to one knee and takes the dog's head in both hands. 'You'll do me proud, won't you, Madeiro?'

The dog licks Nilsen's face.

'We'll see each other again. When all this is over, you'll have been to the pole and back,' Nilsen says brightly. But he knows there's little chance of any of the dogs returning alive.

CHAPTER TWELVE

The sun fills the southern sky with exaggerated brilliance that steadfastly refuses to give way to night. Just as well. The unloading of building materials is in full swing and constant daylight is a godsend. Packing cases pile up on the sea ice beside the ship. Some of the prefabricated sections of the hut are already lashed to a sledge, ready to haul up to the building site 4 kilometres inland. Everyone agrees Amundsen should have the honour of taking the first sledge load. He harnesses his team of eight dogs while the men gather to witness what is to be a symbolic start to their polar quest. This first load weighs a conservative

300 kilograms – but the dogs don't seem to remember what comes next. Even the Three Musketeers sit quietly on the ice, blinking in the bright sunlight.

Amundsen cracks his whip above their heads. Startled into action, the dogs leap to their feet and dash away from the ship. With a triumphant wave to the admiring crew, Amundsen is off. But it doesn't last. The dogs slow to a trot, then stop. Once more they lie down on the ice. There's stifled laughter aboard the *Fram*. Amundsen cracks his whip again and urges them onward with his most commanding voice. This time the dogs launch themselves at each other in a violent explosion of fur and claws and fangs and tangled leather traces.

'Keep it up!' somebody shouts before ducking for cover behind the ship's railing.

Despite feeling foolish for expecting a grand departure, Amundsen can see the humour in the mayhem. It takes four men to bring the situation under control and get the sledge moving again in the right direction. Amundsen's whip does the rest of the work. Hateful as it is, violence is the only encouragement the dogs will recognise in their stop-go-stop-go progress. Howling and protesting, mightily offended by this new harsh treatment, they disappear up the track, with Amundsen and his oscillating whip looking every bit like a conductor leading his orchestra through a challenging piece of music.

Amundsen scrutinises the team. That they're out of shape is to be expected, but it's more than that. They seem confused. The dogs run, slow down, feel the whip, run again. It's a rhythm of sorts, but not one he wants. With this kind of mucking about it'll take a whole year to get to the pole and another to return. Suddenly, it occurs to him – it's the harnesses.

Back at the ship, he discusses the problem. If they're to resolve it quickly, he'll need help.

'What's the difference?' asks Oscar. He has no experience with sledging and he's eager to learn anything he can, given he'll soon be responsible for his own team and his own whip, which he can't ever imagine using.

'Alaskan style has an eight-dog team harnessed to the sledge two by two. It's definitely more balanced, a more efficient way of travelling,' says Amundsen. 'The Greenland style is to have the dogs fanning out from the sledge, running side by side. Unfortunately we have Greenland dogs in Alaskan harnesses.'

Oscar doesn't fully understand. 'Do we need to retrain the dogs?'

Amundsen scoffs. 'No time for that. We'll just have to adapt the harnesses that we've got.' He looks at Sverre. 'What do you think?'

The dog expert shrugs. 'Splice the ropes, alter the tackle. It's definitely possible.'

Amundsen looks at all the equipment piling up around them. 'Well, let's make a start. The sea ice won't hold us forever.'

CHAPTER THIRTEEN

Stubberud throws open the tent flap and swears loudly into the gale. The wind has been tearing at the canvas all night like a bearer of urgent news. With a heavy heart, the carpenter slides the reindeer hood over his head and lumbers out onto the snow.

'It's like we never even dug the holes!' he rages to Bjaaland.

'Bloody wind,' Bjaaland mutters. He kicks around in the snowdrifts that have accumulated over the spot where they left their shovels and pickaxes the night before. His back aches just looking at the hateful tools. A full day of physical exertion followed by a night of fitful sleep. As unpleasant as the sea journey was, Bjaaland wishes he was back in his cabin aboard the *Fram*.

Stubberud grunts, grabs a shovel. It took all day for the two of them to dig foundations a little more than a metre deep. The first half-hour of digging was easy enough, but then they hit ice as hard as granite. Pickaxes replaced shovels. It now appears that all their effort was for nothing.

The site Amundsen has chosen for the hut is on a gentle slope in a wider basin. The hut will have an east–west orientation, with the entrance facing away from the prevailing winds. Even with the slight shelter offered by the incline, the hut needs to be anchored deep. The wind is sure to be even more of a menace during winter.

After five minutes Bjaaland stops shovelling. 'This is hopeless. The holes are filling up quicker than we can empty them out.'

Breathless, Stubberud simply nods. They need a wind-break, some planks or a makeshift wall for the snow to gather behind.

'Even a sledge tipped on its side would do the trick.' Stubberud squints into the distance. 'I wish those lads would hurry up. I'm not walking all the way down to the ship for one.'

The other members of the land party have established a dog camp roughly halfway between the building site and the *Fram*, where everything can be stored safely away from the water's edge and the dogs that are not working can be chained at a safe distance from precious supplies and each other. The view from the dog camp is impressive, taking in the entire Bay of Whales. The *Fram* appears like a toy from this slightly higher vantage point. The 2-kilometre track leading down to the water's edge is marked out with wildly flapping blue flags, an odd sight in the uninhabited desolation of Antarctica. But there's precious little time to stop and admire the view. Many of the loads must continue on to the building site where their base will slowly take shape. Even with the dogs doing most of the pulling, it's physically draining work for the men, travelling into a fierce headwind. Combined with the wind chill, the cold is at times severe. Any work takes twice as long with cumbersome reindeer mitts. While loading and unloading the sledges can be accomplished, any strapping and unstrapping of loads requires lighter gloves or sometimes painfully bare hands.

The three most experienced dog drivers, Sverre, Helmer and Johansen, are hoarse with constant shouting. The whip takes up the cause. Harnessed in the more familiar Greenland style, the dogs still don't always do what's required. They're having too much fun. Having gorged themselves on seal meat the night before then fallen into a deep contented sleep, the dogs have excess energy to burn and leap about at the prospect of running and fighting. Once hitched to the sledge they blast off in multiple directions, narrowly avoiding supplies and stacks of building materials. Sometimes the only way drivers can avoid harm is by overturning the sledge. The scene is one of chaos.

Oscar knows it's only a matter of time before he'll be called on. But for now, he'll do anything to avoid sledging duties. He's seen enough. Only that morning Amundsen was travelling at tremendous speed towards the *Fram* when his dogs caught sight of some seals. The wide arc of the whip was a bad sign; the wild zigzagging course of the sledge a clear indication that the chief had lost control. Mere seconds before plunging headlong into the sea, Amundsen managed to capsize the sledge, the deep, loose snow bringing the madness swiftly to a close. Oscar can't help worrying: if that can happen to the chief, what awful calamities are in store for a rookie like him?

CHAPTER FOURTEEN

'How many is that now?' Sverre rolls the four seal carcasses off the sledge while the dogs tug and jerk at their chains in anticipation of the still-warm meat being dished out.

'Probably a hundred or so,' says Helmer. 'The chief wants at least two hundred to see us through the winter. We've got plenty of penguin. We can probably stop the slaughter of those poor devils.'

'What does penguin taste like anyway?' Sverre asks as he cuts into the seal's belly, releases the innards, and tosses them to the waiting pack of dogs.

Helmer frowns. 'Dunno. Never tasted it. Must be like

duck or goose. There's a fair bit of meat on a penguin. And fat.'

The snow has turned a deep red around the carcasses. Sverre screws up his mouth as he pries open the ribs. 'It doesn't matter how many times you do it. This job is still disgusting,' he grumbles.

Helmer shakes his head. 'I could tell you about disgusting.'

'You don't think I'm a good judge of disgusting? I'm up to my elbows in blood and guts. How about we swap places. I'll stand with my arms crossed and you come and butcher these carcasses.'

Helmer stares into the distance. 'How's this? A Netsilik woman scooping up congealed seal's blood and slurping it from her hands like it's a bowl of cream – that's disgusting. Or children fighting over the fermented fish from the seal's stomach – that's disgusting. How about . . .'

'Helmer, you're not the only one with incredible tales from the Arctic. Remember, I've travelled around Greenland with Sverdrup for three years eating nothing but seal.'

'Well, you should be more than happy,' Helmer chortles. 'This is just like the good old days!'

'Come on, give me a hand,' Sverre says with his knife poised above the ribcage, 'once those guts are gone, I'll be the only thing standing between those dogs and their feed and I'm not quite ready to die.'

Up at the building site, Bjaaland and Stubberud take a moment to admire their handiwork. In just under a week they've patched together the hut they originally built then dismantled in Amundsen's garden in Norway. Attaching the roof and fitting the chimney comes next. They've become good mates during the build, sharing confidences, little jokes about this and that, observations about the others. Amundsen has joined the two men in their camp for the last few nights, keen to ensure everything will fit in the confines of their new accommodation. He's also hoping his presence will keep them to their schedule. Everything must be finished before the *Fram* leaves.

'How much longer, lads?' Amundsen says, shielding his eyes in the sunlight.

There's a squawk. Then another, this time more insistent. An emperor penguin announces itself from behind their tent. His glossy white chest puffed out, the penguin totters forward on its stumpy legs, taking bow after bow like a slightly nervous salesman making a surprise house call.

Bjaaland delights in seeing the stunning creature in such close quarters. A true South Pole native come to say hello. More bowing. The penguin totters closer. Another squawk. More bowing. Closer. He seems intent on introducing himself to his new neighbours. Bjaaland doesn't notice Stubberud approach from behind with the hammer in his hand. One swift strike ends it all. The penguin tips over, dead.

Bjaaland gasps. 'What did you do that for?'

'Look at these flippers – powerful weapons. They'd break a man's back.' Stubberud gives the penguin another blow to the head to make sure the job's done properly. He doesn't want to skin an animal that's merely stunned.

'Good job,' says Amundsen plainly.

'But we have food,' says Bjaaland.

Stubberud shrugs and looks at the chief, hoping he'll explain the unpleasant stuff.

'You can't afford to be sentimental, Bjaaland. Not here,' says Amundsen. 'We have 110 dogs and nine men to feed for a year.'

'I just think it's . . .'

Stubberud grins. 'You didn't care so much about the seals.'

Bjaaland stares at the penguin, loose necked with the few dots of blood now stark against the snow. 'But he was just trying to be friendly, to say hello.'

Stubberud snorts. 'You big softie. What will you think when we have to start killing off the dogs?'

Bjaaland's jaw drops.

'Yes well, nothing pleasant about that,' says Amundsen with a sigh.

'So why do it?'

'Necessity. We're covering such a distance, we won't be able to carry enough food for both us and the dogs. Even with supply depots. Some of the dogs will have to be sacrificed.'

'Not willingly,' murmurs Bjaaland.

Amundsen's response is blunt. 'We must be successful. There is no conceivable alternative.' What he doesn't say is that if he ventures back to Norway without securing the South Pole victory, his career might well be over, having lied to the king, Nansen and the nation. The men's reputations will be tainted too. No further philosophising is necessary: either he succeeds or he dies trying.

Back and forth, back and forth. The dogs work in five-hour shifts. The men put in twelve-hour days in order to get everything organised. Nine hundred crates in total, each one stacked with its unique number facing outwards so its contents can be matched against Amundsen's master list. He's spent years researching and planning his supplies. How much food will each man need per kilometre of distance he travels? What kind of food – more dry biscuits, or greater quantities of preserved meat? And what will the dogs eat? How much will it weigh and how much energy will it deliver? Will they have enough to last them if bad weather waylays their progress? What's a reasonable margin of safety? Amundsen's calculations don't just revolve around planning meals either. The performance of skis and bindings has been studied and perfected. Sledges have been modified and made as light as possible without compromising their strength. Clothing and sleeping bags and tents have been chosen to withstand the worst wind, lowest temperatures and wear and tear of a southern journey that will last months. Everything has been thought through to the smallest detail and tested once, twice, three times before leaving Norway. All the while Amundsen reads and re-reads the published accounts by Captain Scott and Ernest Shackleton of their time spent in Antarctica. But rather than seeking answers, the Norwegian pores over the texts for lessons in what went wrong. Whatever he can learn from the failure of others might save his life and the lives of his men.

Has Scott taken such a scientific approach to logistics? Amundsen cannot concern himself with how well others have planned. It is utterly out of his control and therefore pointless. He does worry about Scott's famed motor sledges, however. More than once he's imagined Captain Scott's mechanical wonders, chugging all the way to the pole while the Norwegians attempt a world first with a wild pack of dogs and skis strapped to their feet.

1898 – THE BELGICA EXPEDITION

Two men are already dead. Another two have been driven insane by their predicament. Most of the crew are suffering from cramps and lethargy, with the blackened gums, loose teeth and foul breath of scurvy. Few have the energy or mental strength to even leave their bunks. De Gerlache himself has locked his cabin door, surrendering to black thoughts.

First mate Amundsen can see it now. An accident? No. It was always the intention of the commander to trap the ship in the ice, to drift amid the uncharted southern reaches of the Bellingshausen Sea just so he could boast of being the first to overwinter in Antarctica. Like it or not, they are all prisoners of an ice field that extends into hundreds of kilometres of nothingness. In all likelihood they will not survive the ordeal. De Gerlache is an inexperienced fool. Amundsen knows the Belgica is ill-equipped and under-provisioned. Nobody has winter clothes, there is scarcely enough paraffin to burn two lamps and yet several months of darkness are already upon them. Water seeps down the inside of the hull, and a damp cold invades the ship and deprives the crew of even the most modest comforts – a warm bed, dry clothes. Fear gnaws away at the men in the endless night. Might they drift forever with no prospect of rescue? No one has any energy left for fighting. Depression has taken over from aggression aboard the Belgica.

'You're my kind of man, Amundsen,' says the ship's surgeon Dr Cook, one of the few men aboard with polar experience. Cook is courageous, calm and wise in the ways of survival. He all but assumes control of the ship. Amundsen and Cook busy themselves hunting to supplement rations, making brief forays beyond the ship in the dim light, working tirelessly to improve their inadequate equipment and clothing. Against the commander's orders, Cook force-feeds the seal and penguin meat to the scurvy-stricken crew. The peculiar flavour offends but ultimately saves lives. De Gerlache finally relents, but only when death is the alternative.

Twenty-six years old and Amundsen's hair has turned grey. Lucky it didn't fall out. He has filled five notebooks with his detailed analysis of the expedition's failings. It's not for sharing or for seeking damages. It's for nobody's benefit but his own. Experience was what he was after; an education is what he received.

CHAPTER FIFTEEN

Nobody dares mention how tiny their hut is – a mere eight by four metres. It's certainly roomier than the tents the men have been sleeping in for almost a month. Eight members of the land party cluster around the dining table amid the comforting smells emanating from the kitchen. Lindstrøm is cooking their first meal on his new coal range. The men look scruffy and out of place in the shiny new home they have christened 'Framheim'. Ruddy faces, chapped lips and crusty cheeks are a natural consequence of weeks spent working in fierce wind and bone-dry air. Now would be the time to grow facial hair, the thicker the better, but Amundsen, convinced that a tidy appearance encourages other tidy habits, has decreed that each man must shave once a week.

'Last time we saw this little house it was sitting in your garden on the Bunde Fjord, surrounded by trees, the air full of birdsong,' says Prestrud.

'What's wrong with ice?' Stubberud says with mock astonishment.

'We also have snow,' suggests Bjaaland playfully.

'And I'll give you birdsong.' Helmer starts to make the loud buzzing squawk of an emperor penguin but he's soon shouted down by the rest of the party.

'Here's to unique beauty, wherever we may find it,' Amundsen says, raising a toast. 'To Framheim!'

'*Skål!*' The men pledge their friendship, clink their glasses and brace themselves for the back-of-the-throat sting of the aquavit. Johansen nurses a mug of tea and a grimace but does his best to meet each toast with good grace. Rousing music from the gramophone sets the tone. The men raise a cheer to Framheim, to their leader, to the successful completion of their journey and to the safe return of the *Fram* once it's all over. Good humour and optimism unify the men on their first night. The dogs, now fastened to wire ropes stretched in a large open square outside, start their nightly concert. First one, then a couple, then the entire congregation start up in their howling chorus, sitting low to the ground with their heads extended skyward.

'What makes them do that?' Oscar asks Amundsen.

'Ask Sverre. He knows dogs best.'

Sverre blushes, pleased that the chief defers to his superior knowledge. 'Actually, no one knows why they do that. Why they start up. Why they stop so suddenly. The strangest thing I find is that they all stop at exactly the same time. No stragglers. Not one dog decides to carry on as a soloist.'

'Well, we know they're expert communicators,' says Amundsen. 'They have different voices for different purposes. One for fighting, one for playing, an entirely different voice when things are wrong, when they see one of their kind breaking the rules. It's like a child running to teacher to tell on his classmates.'

'That sound reminds me of wolves howling,' says Bjaaland.

'Not far removed from wolves,' says Sverre. 'Everything they do is based on the pecking order. They all know their place.'

'And man needs to be at the top of the pack.' Amundsen is keen to emphasise this to the novices. 'If he's not at the top, then he is actually at the bottom.'

'I've noticed,' Oscar sighs. Both he and Prestrud have spent the last week coming to grips with the basics of driving a dog team. He hates using the whip but experience has taught him that he must establish himself as leader or face being taken for a ride. Lieutenant Prestrud has encountered exactly the same challenge but is more open to dominating his team through the use of physical force. Everyone assumes he's the sensible one, the quiet, studious navigational expert, peering at his instruments, taking his readings. But it's obvious to all who see Prestrud flash by that driving a dog team is more raucous fun than the lieutenant has had in almost a whole decade in the Norwegian Navy.

Amundsen is clearly fascinated by dogs. He wriggles closer to the table. 'You know I could take the meat from the mouths of my sledge dogs and not one of them would dare bite me. I'd never try that trick on one of my house dogs. I'd likely lose a finger.'

After the laughter dies down Bjaaland looks across the table and asks, 'How about you, Johansen? What's your experience of dogs?'

Johansen shifts in his seat, adjusts his grip on his mug of tea and opens his mouth to speak.

However, Amundsen interrupts. 'Excuse me, Johansen, but I think we need to get down to business.'

Johansen forces a smile. Obviously the time for stories has passed.

'But dinner is ready,' Lindstrøm insists. He has extremely high standards of punctuality.

Amundsen looks up at the cook with an indulgent smile and says, 'I won't be long, Fatty.'

Lindstrøm nods, wipes his hands on the cloth at his waist and retreats back to the kitchen.

'Our goal lies at 90 degrees south, approximately 1100 kilometres away. We shall be racing against time and starvation. Now that we have established Framheim at 78 degrees south, it is imperative that we start to lay supply depots along our proposed route. One supply depot for every degree of latitude. That's roughly 100 kilometres apart, or as far as we can get them before winter sets in. I want to start preparing for this immediately.'

Lindstrøm taps the palm of his hand with a soup ladle in a sign of exaggerated impatience. Amundsen continues, 'I will need each man to do his part with the dog teams.'

Oscar grimaces self-consciously. 'I don't think I . . .'

Amundsen raises his palms, asking for patience. 'Four men will accompany three sledges and eighteen dogs. Others can pack and secure the provisions. I've calculated 250 kilograms per sledge with each load forming a depot.'

'I'd like to volunteer,' says Helmer.

'And me,' says Prestrud, eager for some real-life sledging experience.

Johansen slowly puts up his hand, half expecting his offer of help to be dismissed, but it's not.

'Excellent,' says Amundsen.

'Can I bring in the stew now?' Lindstrøm asks.

Amundsen gestures at the table. 'You may.'

There's a knock at the entrance to the hut.

'Our first visitor,' says Lindstrøm, plonking the heavy casserole on the table. 'Wanting to see where the good smells are coming from.'

In fact it's Lieutenant Gjertsen from the *Fram*, looking like he's over-exerted himself on his dash up the hill. Lindstrøm ushers him in and takes his coat but the lieutenant doesn't wish to sit. He tries to catch his breath. 'There's another sailing ship in the bay. Captain Nilsen says it's the *Terra Nova*. Scott's expedition ship. Sir, it's the English.'

CHAPTER SIXTEEN

The *Terra Nova* is a mess. Filthy inside and out. Amundsen smiles as the captain of the English ship welcomes him below decks in a show of hospitality. He decides to keep his uncharitable thoughts to himself. The last thing he wants to do is cause offence in a foreign language.

Lunch in the ship's wardroom is a simple affair. Canned vegetables, mutton and some hard savoury cakes the English call 'scones'. It's a friendly gesture, one that Amundsen, Captain Nilsen and Lieutenant Prestrud appreciate. They showed the Englishmen around Framheim that morning. Of the three Norwegians, Nilsen has the best command of English, although Amundsen and Prestrud both speak it well enough to be shocked by the nature of the mealtime conversation.

'It rained down like mustard!' laughs Lieutenant Pennell, commander of the *Terra Nova*. 'Onto the table, while the men were eating their dinner!'

Lieutenant Victor Campbell shakes his head at the recollection. 'Absolutely disgusting – it left a frightful mess for the chaps to clean up.'

Amundsen's mouth twists in distaste. 'Manure from the ponies onto this table?'

'Yes, their stalls were directly overhead.' Campbell points to the brown staining on the white painted ceiling.

Pennell roars with laughter. 'We had so much water sloshing about up there on deck. The manure seeped down into the men's sleeping quarters too.'

'We had our own muck to worry about,' says Captain Nilsen. 'One hundred dogs can produce quite a lot. We all had accidents. Our chief included . . .'

Amundsen waves away Nilsen's invitation to tell the tale. Such conversation is a waste of precious time. What he really wants to know is, *do the English have radio*, a way of transmitting news to the outside world. Just thinking of the dreadful consequences of Cook and Peary both claiming victory at the North Pole, he realises it's a situation remarkably like his own: two men striving for the same goal, winner takes all. Amundsen understands perfectly the advantage access to a radio transmitter would afford Captain Scott.

'First time in Antarctica?' Campbell offers Amundsen a cigarette.

Amundsen declines. He stopped smoking back in September in preparation for the polar journey. 'No, I was here before. With de Gerlache aboard the *Belgica*.'

Campbell nods. 'That Belgian expedition?'

'There were some Norwegians, Polish, a Romanian, an American. But mostly Belgians.'

'How long were you in Antarctica?'

'Fifteen months. Our ship was trapped in the ice for most of that.'

'How ghastly,' simpers Lieutenant Pennell. 'I do hope the same does not happen to our vessels.'

Amundsen raises his chin and sucks in his cheeks in an expression neither Englishman can read.

Campbell narrows his eyes. 'The American you mention. That was Dr Cook – the Arctic explorer? Seems a damn shame, this whole fiasco with Robert Peary. Both men claiming to be first to reach the North Pole. Though goodness knows if Cook even got there.'

Amundsen shakes his head emphatically. 'I am sorry, I cannot hear bad things of Dr Cook.'

'Gosh,' says Pennell, slightly taken aback.

'Cook is a very courageous man. A good friend.'

'There you have it, Pennell,' says Campbell, slapping his thighs with a levity designed to turn the afternoon's conversation back to more frivolous topics.

After several hours of friendly conversation below deck in the dark interior, the harsh light of day leaves them all blinking at each other, suddenly reminded of their rivalry.

'Fine vessel, Lieutenant,' Amundsen remarks to Campbell as they walk the length of the deck. Amundsen shields his eyes against the sun as he glances surreptitiously at the rigging, searching for any sign of a radio aerial.

'This is where the ponies were housed.' Campbell points at the filthy stalls that give off a rank odour even though the ponies were offloaded weeks ago.

'A long journey for such large animals, no?' Amundsen says mildly. 'All survived?'

'We lost two. The result of the storm just after we left New Zealand. We also lost a couple of dogs. One washed overboard, the other hanged on its chain.'

Amundsen nods in silent acknowledgement. Both men know the perils of long sea voyages. 'How many ponies do you have?'

'Nineteen,' says Campbell. 'And thirty dogs. And three motor sledges.'

'And how are the motor sledges going on the snow?' Amundsen hopes not to sound too inquisitive.

'Extremely well. We have high hopes they'll prove to be very useful.' Campbell doesn't mention that of the three motor sledges, one lies on the bottom of McMurdo Sound and one has already broken down. Instead he changes the subject. 'And how about you, what's the extent of your animal contingent?'

'We have just over a hundred dogs. And twenty puppies born at sea.'

Campbell widens his eyes in interest.

'They'll be big enough by the time spring arrives.'

'So you have placed *all* your faith in dogs then?' Perhaps Campbell is fishing for clues as to what the Norwegians have planned. Amundsen is practised at such games of cat and mouse and knows just how much to disclose.

'Norwegians are good skiers. With skis on our feet and dogs to pull our sledges, we are hopeful of a fast trip to the pole and back.'

Campbell gives a weak laugh. 'Yes, you certainly have speed on your side.'

Campbell is referring to the morning's display of sledging prowess. Amundsen is pleased it did not go unnoticed. Campbell will undoubtedly report back to Captain Scott how the Norwegians had blazed down the trail from Framheim to the edge of the bay, the dogs running like a pack of hungry wolves – an impressive sight.

'What are your plans now?' asks Amundsen.

The lieutenant breathes in deeply. 'We had hoped to journey eastward to the furthermost edge of the Great Ice Barrier to reach King Edward VII Land, but sea ice bars the way. With you Norwegians based here at the Bay of Whales, which was to be our Plan B, we shall have to come up with a Plan C and find some other location to explore.'

'You're welcome to join us. You could make your base on the barrier as we have.'

'No, I think we'll head back west towards McMurdo. We don't want to cause any more bother.'

Amundsen nods. 'I understand, you must make the most of your time before leaving for civilisation.'

'That reminds me,' says Campbell. 'Do you have any mail? We could send it when we reach New Zealand.'

'That is a kind offer, Lieutenant. But we have no major achievements to report. At least not yet.'

Lieutenant Campbell doesn't respond to Amundsen's playful remark. Of course it is a huge disappointment to find the Norwegians occupying the Bay of Whales, where he and his six-man team had hoped to base themselves in order to explore the Great Ice Barrier. When the two parties bid farewell, neither feels aggrieved. It's been more a meeting of colleagues than arch rivals. But the moment he steps off the *Terra Nova*, Amundsen turns to Prestrud and Captain Nilsen and asks in Norwegian, 'Any sign the Englishmen have a radio?'

Prestrud glances back at the sailing ship. Nobody is within earshot. 'None that I saw – and the men guided me over the entire vessel. Could be hidden in a cupboard.'

'No aerial,' says Nilsen, pulling his cap down and putting an end to any speculation once and for all.

'Would they go so far as to hide it? Take down the aerial?' Amundsen is beginning to sound paranoid. He purses his lips and casts his eyes once more over the *Terra Nova*. Nilsen is correct. Both the English and Norwegians will have to sail to the nearest inhabited land to convey any official announcement to the world.

Amundsen pauses to reflect on the visit, the conversations, the behaviour of the various crew members they met. 'They were very nice,' he thinks aloud. 'But they seemed far more interested in finding out about our plans than disguising their own.'

Captain Nilsen says, 'The vessel was rather basic, wasn't it? Grubby. And as for the pony manure dripping down from the stables – I'm not sure our crew would have put up with that.'

Prestrud mumbles agreement. 'Enough to put me off Lindstrøm's pancakes in the morning.'

'We're going to miss those when we cast off,' grumbles Nilsen. 'We'll have nothing exciting to look forward to after a night's watch.'

'Can't be helped,' Amundsen says without a glimmer of pity. 'My boys will be in need of him most. One thing I've learnt over the years is the importance of good food. If men can't look forward to a fine meal at the end of the day, nothing will keep their spirits up over a long winter. Fatty will be feeding our souls, not just our stomachs.'

CHAPTER SEVENTEEN

A tiny village in the vast shimmering emptiness, that is what Framheim resembles by the first weeks of February. Fourteen tents have sprung up around the main hut like pale-capped mushrooms. Eight provide shelter for the dog teams, somewhere to hunker down at night and escape the penetrating cold. Oscar and Bjaaland have dug out the snow beneath each tent so that the dogs have a sunken lair, which provides additional insulation while protecting the tent canvas from sharp teeth and claws.

Another tent provides storage for the men's reindeer clothing and sleeping bags, which need to be kept cold and dry; another holds coal reserves and firewood. One tent has been christened the 'maternity hospital' and offers a little peace and quiet for any dog expecting a litter of puppies. Keeping newborn pups a safe distance from the other dogs is important now that they all roam free during the day. Hauling sledges is hungry work and they've done a great deal in the last few weeks. The dogs are ravenous and will eat anything they find lying around. The tent they use to store the seal meat and dried fish has a wall of snow around it so high it can deter even the most intrepid four-legged thief. There are plenty that will try their luck. Madeiro, Captain Nilsen's pup, even sneaked into Lindstrøm's kitchen and stole a side of beef.

Amundsen inspects the layout of the camp with Prestrud, who has taken a break from his navigational tables in the hope that the chill air will clear his mind. For hours he's sat hunched at the table in the hut, his head swimming with figures, astronomical data, calculations and observations he must make sense of in order to plot the supply depots. Prestrud feels like the only thing he ever does is flick back and forth through the pages of his Nautical Almanac for 1911, which lists the position of the sun and moon and a whole range of celestial bodies for every hour of every day for an entire year. With this information at his fingertips, a chronometer to tell the exact time, and a sextant to measure the angle of the sun from the horizon, Prestrud will be able to establish their position relative to the pole at every stage of their journey. While Amundsen and Johansen have their own navigational experience and Prestrud has attempted to impart some rudimentary knowledge to the others, it is his head on the chopping block should an error occur.

Both men are still fighting off the head cold passed on by the Englishmen during their visit to the *Terra Nova*. Amundsen stops, his face screwed up as if contemplating a horrible thought. He stays like that, head raised, his hooked nose twitching in expectation. Finally he faces into the sun and releases a loud, satisfying sneeze. 'Excuse me.'

Staring at the ground, Prestrud barely registers the apology. He has something terrible to own up to and he's put off telling the chief for weeks. He knows he can no longer keep it to himself. 'Sir, I've got bad news.'

'Mmmm?' Amundsen bends down to ruffle the heads of the Three Musketeers, who have bounded over for some attention. Amundsen is temporarily consumed by the task of scratching ears.

Prestrud waits to the side, nudging away other dogs that come looking for a dose of human kindness. He swallows hard. 'I forgot to bring the Nautical Almanac for 1912.'

Amundsen doesn't hear. He's engaged in conversation with one of the growling dogs. 'You're a bit too greedy, aren't you? Pushing the others out of the way to squeeze closer to me so I'll give you a rub – don't you know there's plenty for all of you? Plenty of rubbing and patting and . . .'

Prestrud can't be sure Amundsen heard him. 'Sir.'

Amundsen straightens up his hood and gives a deep sniff. 'Yes, the Nautical Almanac,' he says, suddenly serious and fixing Prestrud with his penetrating gaze. 'You forgot it.'

'I left it. It's back in Norway. I just don't know how I managed to . . .'

Amundsen doesn't speak. He takes a long hard look at the lieutenant without blinking, seemingly without breathing. Finally he says, 'Then we shall have to reach the pole by the end of the year, won't we?'

This is not the angry response Prestrud expected. Momentarily confused, he sets off on a tumbling diagnosis of the situation that led to its being left.

The light touch of Amundsen's hand on his forearm stops Prestrud mid-sentence. 'It's alright. I know you'll make do with what you've got. By the way, how many copies of the Almanac for 1911 do you have?'

Prestrud blushes. 'One.'

Amundsen raises his eyebrows. 'Then we'll have to be especially careful with it, won't we?'

'I've made six copies of the navigational tables,' the lieutenant says hurriedly.

'Very good. And how many do you plan to take on the depot-laying journey?'

Prestrud pauses. Is it a trick question? 'Two?' he offers sheepishly.

Amundsen shrugs his shoulders. 'You're our navigator. If you want two, take two. Frankly I don't care if you leave all your navigational tables at home and set fire to our only copy of the Nautical Almanac as long as you can guide us to the pole and back in the fastest possible time.'

Prestrud grimaces. Amundsen's comment is not so much a vote of confidence as a thinly veiled ultimatum.

Chapter Eighteen

Amundsen takes a moment to catch his breath. From this vantage point the *Fram* appears a dark speck, Framheim a slightly larger smudge due to the nearsightedness Amundsen refuses to acknowledge. Turning from the Bay of Whales, he focuses his attention on what lies before him – the unknown continent. His smile is infectious. Prestrud, Johansen and Helmer grin back.

'What are you waiting for?' he calls to Prestrud. 'Lead on!'

Prestrud sets off in a southerly direction, his long narrow skis moving effortlessly across the hard-packed surface. Helmer gives him a five-minute head start before urging his dogs to follow across the empty plain. The other two teams are keen to get going but Johansen is careful to leave a distance of a hundred metres or so between his six dogs and Helmer's. Any man who has experienced the headache of untangling two dog teams engaged in an all-out war will know that it's easier to avoid conflict than resolve it. Finally, Amundsen readies his dogs and sets them after the other teams, each of them ably hauling 250 kilograms of supplies towards the unresolved horizon. The chief checks the distance-meter, a wheel extending behind his sledge that will keep count of the kilometres they cover. It turns again and again, its steady accumulation of metres proof of their progress in a banal white landscape devoid of natural features or points of reference. His thoughts travel widely, but his eyes remain trained on the unbroken tracks extending before him. It's only a matter of time before he'll need to scoop up some article dropped by somebody up ahead.

'A little to the right!' shouts Helmer.

Prestrud alters his course slightly without responding. Nobody envies his job. It is tedious, lonely and psychologically taxing to act as a 'forerunner', providing something for the dogs to follow in the otherwise blank scene.

'A little to the left!' shouts Helmer.

Prestrud turns abruptly. Even without seeing his expression clearly, Helmer knows the filthy look directed back at him. He points in an exaggerated manner at his compass. How can he help it if Prestrud deviates from their southerly bearing? He should count himself lucky. Keeping an eye on a team of dogs is far trickier, figuring out who's working and who's shirking, and keeping the sledge from capsizing on the uneven terrain. Helmer checks his compass and mutters in exasperation. Once again he shouts: 'A little to the right.'

Prestrud focuses on the rhythmic sound his skis make on the thin layer of loose snow. He is the first ever human being to make tracks here. It's a nice thought, but is it enough to keep him going over hours, days and weeks of monotony?

The four men proceed at a rattling pace. Snow conditions are perfect and the dogs are performing well. But even though the weather is calm and mild, soon a grey haze settles around them, causing everything to appear flat and the land and sky to merge into blankness. The effect is disorientating and snow goggles provide little relief. With no shadows to indicate contours in the white surface, something as simple as keeping upright becomes a great challenge. Prestrud tips over time and again. He feels foolish, even though the others stumble too, momentarily caught off guard by an imperceptible hump or hollow. At least they're able to grab hold of a sledge and steady themselves. Prestrud is sick of scrambling to his feet.

The men pitch camp late in the afternoon, satisfied with the 15 kilometres they've travelled since their 9.30 departure. Two tents, each accommodating two men, spring up in the white while the dogs settle down in the snow, delighting in their blocks of frozen fish meal and fat.

Inside one of the tents, Amundsen and Helmer start the evening's food preparations. There's a knack to lighting the Primus burner and it takes Amundsen a few minutes to get the paraffin flowing in the cold. Meanwhile, Helmer has loaded up the Nansen cooker with snow, whistling a cheerful tune as he works. The cooker has two parts – an inner chamber for cooking the meal and an outer chamber for melting snow to make hot chocolate. Once the snow has melted in the inner chamber, Helmer stirs in a crumbled block of pemmican. Only a few stirs and the dried meat and fat melt into the boiling water. Dinner is served. They won't all eat together. There's not enough room. Johansen and Prestrud will need to scuttle into the other tent and eat before the warming effect is lost to the surrounding chill.

The cooker has warmed the air in Amundsen and Helmer's tent, for a time at least. Both men have removed their boots and stripped off their heavy outer layers, which hasn't been easy in such a confined space. Dinnertime conversation is confined to tired grunts. Wriggling down into their reindeer sleeping bags feels like the ultimate luxury, despite still being clad in a full set of clothes. Feet and hands are covered and a hood is drawn tight over their heads. The temperature outside is a brisk minus seven.

Amundsen wakes. He lies there blinking for a moment, his eyes trying to focus on the white fabric overhead. All this daylight. *Where am I?* His breath clouds, complicating things. Helmer is snoring – back to his old tricks. The noise brings Amundsen back to the two-man tent, to depot-laying, to Antarctica.

'Helmer!' Amundsen fumbles with the drawstring under his chin, releasing his head. Frigid air floods into his sleeping bag, chasing the remnants of sleep from his system. With the efficiency that comes from years of practice Amundsen pulls his reindeer-skin anorak on over his head, slips his legs from the bag and into his reindeer trousers and guides his feet into his fur kamiks. 'Helmer Hansen!' he shouts.

The snoring continues unabated. Amundsen unfastens the tent flap and sticks his head out into the bright sunlight. The almost acid sharpness of the air displaces the stale fug of the tent. He breathes deeply, enjoying the cleansing burn of it in his lungs. A few dogs lift their heads in the direction of the sound. A number spring to their feet as his figure emerges onto the snow and crosses to the second tent. 'Time to get up!' Amundsen shakes one of the guy lines. The canvas offers a hollow reply in the stillness but without much delay there's movement from within, and the ball of a head, pressed against the cloth. Johansen appears a few moments later.

'Morning,' he says, nodding at Amundsen. He wanders beyond the dogs, amid much barking, and relieves himself. There's no shyness among them and certainly no privacy in such wide open spaces. More often than not the dogs will clean up any human mess left on the snow. Hungry dogs are anything but fussy.

'Helmer!' bellows Amundsen.

Helmer stirs from sleep. One eye open, he frowns at the daylight. None too delicately, Amundsen throws open the tent flaps and yanks his empty sleeping bag from next to Helmer and slings it onto the closest sledge. Helmer's punishment will be getting dressed in a wash of cold air.

'Breakfast,' Amundsen says, setting up the Nansen cooker as the other man fumbles out of bed and into his outdoor clothing. It's not a friendly suggestion. Prestrud and Johansen are already folding their bedding away. Helmer needs to pee but there's clean snow to gather into the cooker, hot chocolate to make, the ration bag to unpack. The hiss of the Primus is another hint. He needs to sharpen up his act.

They're on the road at 7.45 a.m. More than three hours to break camp and get the dogs organised. It's too long.

Helmer's dawdling, that's the only reason. Amundsen casts his eye around the area of trampled snow. Satisfied that they have not forgotten anything, he gives the signal. Once again Prestrud strides out on the Antarctic plain. Helmer turns and salutes like a soldier entering battle. Amundsen cannot stay mad at him – the truth is, with his humour, his knight-like fealty and their years of shared experience, Helmer's worth a thousand men.

1903 – Ogchotku, Northwest Passage

The five men appear from nowhere. Arctic barbarians. Helmer loads his rifle. Amundsen too. But the friendly greeting of 'Manik-tu-mi! Manik-tu-mi!' puts paid to all threat of hostilities.

Two full winters the Norwegians stay. The Netsilik are good-natured, handsome – families mostly – and curious to see the first white faces to appear in these lonely northern regions in over a century. Soon a whole village of igloos surrounds the Gjøa. Learning to build them takes patience but the Netsilik prove excellent teachers. The Norwegians have a stilted language, strange food and poor clothing. The Netsilik men teach them hunting, survival in deep cold and how to run dog teams. The Netsilik women give them reindeer outfits, loose layers offering warmth and comfort without trapping moisture and sweat. Having experienced the limitations of his woollens, Amundsen needs no convincing about the superiority of the Netsilik clothing. He will come to rely on it. They all will.

The Netsilik dog is skinny. Amundsen has seen how it roves about the camp, whining, wolfing down human excrement in the absence of any other sustenance. It growls as Amundsen approaches his master's igloo. He is loyal even when there is no food.

Amundsen has brought bread, Lindstrøm's friendship offering to their Netsilik companions, who are constantly offering gifts, wildlife specimens he will take back for the museum in Norway. Lindstrøm's collection has grown to include Arctic birds, foxes, rabbits, even ticks and lice picked off human bodies. The work keeps him busy and he is always stuffing and mounting some beast on the big chart table aboard the ship.

The bread comes straight from the oven and is wrapped in a cloth. The Netsilik children are first to gather around the curiosity. 'Fatty made it for you,' says Amundsen, miming Lindstrøm's girth and puffing out his cheeks.

Magito, one of the Netsilik women, touches the loaf. The skin of her hand is dark with an accumulation of dried blood from cutting up seal meat, but her fingers are spotlessly clean, the result of much licking. She has a beautiful smile.

Steam rises when Amundsen cuts the first slice. The children finger the white interior, laughing at the strange texture, soft like the underbelly fur of a reindeer. Amundsen tears a corner off and chews it slowly, making appreciative noises and challenging the onlookers to do the same. Magito is quick to follow. Her piece is large and misshapen; it disappears into her mouth. Her eyes grow large. She scuttles outside where sounds of retching and anguished cries can be heard. Nobody moves until she returns. Cross words spill from her mouth. Their meaning is clear: you tried to poison me!

Amundsen protests. Again he slips a knob of bread into his mouth and chews. The children, the women chatter and point and Magito repeats her angry outburst, this time gripping her stomach in a melodramatic fashion. Amundsen decides it's best to retreat.

'Are you surprised, Fatty? No such thing as bread in the Arctic Circle,' Amundsen dismisses Lindstrøm's hurt feelings. 'Only one thing will keep you warm in minus twenty and that's seal meat and blubber.'

A boy they call Dalonakto has come aboard the Gjøa. The Netsilik often do. Making a show of his bravery, Dalonakto bites into the offending loaf and stares with defiance at Helmer.

When the thaw comes and it is time to move on, it is this boy who refuses to leave the boat, even though he must. There is no room, not enough food. Still Dalonakto insists he will join the Norwegians on their navigation of the Northwest Passage.

Helmer's had enough. He points to Dalonakto then to Lindstrøm's stuffed Arctic specimens. 'You, next!' he says pointedly. The boy does not linger.

'A bit of a cruel joke,' Lindstrøm says as they farewell their Netsilik hosts.

Helmer grunts. 'Even if we had managed to chase him off the boat, he would have followed in a sea kayak until we had no choice but take him with us.'

'Don't you see?' says Amundsen sagely. 'With all we've learnt from these folk, we are taking him with us. We're taking all of them with us. Not in body but definitely in spirit.'

CHAPTER NINETEEN

The Norwegians know nothing of what lies ahead of them and what natural obstacles could hamper their progress. All of it is virgin territory, uncharted. One thing is for sure, however: the surface of the eastern barrier is proving ideal for the dogs. Amundsen thinks back to all he has read about Antarctic conditions. Shackleton and Scott have both written about how unsuited dogs are to travel here. How wrong they were! Amundsen can't help feeling he has been misled by their descriptions of the treacherous, demanding conditions. If anything could be improved, it's the sledges – they're way heavier and more rigid than they need to be.

Their third day out from Framheim is marked by thick fog and a distinct impression that they are proceeding downhill. When the fog finally lifts, towards midday, the men find themselves staring at a towering landmass rising from the line of the southern horizon. Out in front, Prestrud points to the horizon in alarm. The harder he works his skis to get a closer look, the further away the land seems to get. The effect is maddening.

Amundsen chuckles to himself. It may look every bit as solid as a mountain but the simple fact is that the dark mass is nothing but a bank of fog, slowly retreating. Prestrud doesn't believe it for a minute when Amundsen enlightens him. He's convinced himself that he's heading for dark foothills, skiing there alone, leading everyone onward. Nobody pushes the point. The next morning when they rise at 4 a.m., the day offers calm, clear conditions.

'Where did my foothills go?' Prestrud gasps amid much hilarity.

It's a surprise to all of them that even in temperatures well below zero, the reindeer sledging outfits are too warm to bother with. Proceeding in underclothes with a wind layer is more than enough to keep the men comfortable during the day, given the exercise they're getting. The dogs pull and the men ski beside them – everybody is working well and the daily distances are covered easily in the six hours of travel they have set themselves. Not far now and they'll have reached their target of 80 degrees south. There is still no sign of any crevasses. Prestrud would be first to encounter any such hazard but with skis over two metres long, it's unlikely he'd fall in or fall far. The dog teams are far more likely to be the first casualties with their dainty paws and compact bodies.

On the fourth day Amundsen comes to the conclusion that their theodolite is not working as it should, making it impossible to position the supply depot in a way that is astronomically accurate. Getting the depot coordinates right is critical if they are to find it again in a vast emptiness the size of France. A combination of regular readings from the compass and the distance meter will have to do. Amundsen has been marking the route with bamboo flagpoles every 15 kilometres, which should be sufficient in conditions of good visibility, but when thick fog settles or the wind whips up the loose snow to the height of a man, it will be another story. They may have to come up with some other system.

It's 11 a.m. on 14 February when Amundsen calls a halt. Minus 19 degrees and still. The dogs pant in confusion, their breath showing up as an aura of white. They don't seem to understand that this is as far as they will travel. For now.

'Eighty degrees south?' asks Helmer.

Amundsen takes off his dark glasses and peers closely at the reading on the sledge-meter to make triple sure. He nods. 'By my reckoning.'

Signalling his relief, Prestrud sends a plume of hot breath skyward.

The men take to their task with great enthusiasm, unfastening the ropes on the sledges and calling out the contents of the crates as they stack them neatly around a central flagpole so Amundsen can note everything down. There are twelve cases of dog pemmican weighing almost half a tonne, 30 kilos of seal steaks and 50 kilos of blubber that the dogs seem particularly interested in. Johansen's whip dissuades them. Two boxes of sledging biscuits, twenty packets of chocolate and a box of margarine top off the 12-foot structure. More will be added when the men return to establish further depots at 82 and 83 degrees south, but for now the hard part is over. With the sledges largely empty, the men face a rather leisurely return to Framheim – this time as passengers.

Helmer breaks up a few empty packing cases to use as markers on their way back.

'Is that all we have?' asks Johansen. 'That's not nearly enough.'

'What else do we have?' says Helmer, exasperated at how well Johansen can point out a problem without offering a solution. 'Shall I cut up your skis?'

'You can cut up my ski boots, they're bloody killing me,' Johansen grumbles.

'Take mine too,' says Prestrud. 'They're so damn stiff. My heels are one big blister.'

'Use these.' Amundsen points to the bundle of dried fish on one of the sledges. 'Even if we can't see the route, the dogs will sniff it out.'

'We've got plenty.' Helmer pauses while he makes a rough calculation. 'Enough for every 250 metres or so.'

In the end it's Amundsen's job to stick a dried fish into the snow every time Prestrud gives the signal. With their old tracks to follow home, Prestrud is no longer needed to blaze a trail out front. Sitting on the back of the last sledge with one eye on the slow turn of the sledge-meter, he contemplates the empty landscape. Pride swells in his chest. It wasn't so bad to act as frontrunner. In fact, to be the first man to venture into the new land was an honour. Now as they return northward, Prestrud has the luxury of being the last man to take it all in. The view south looks somewhat different than when he set out towards it. What was virgin snow is now a jumble of sledge tracks and paw prints, punctuated by the neat parallel lines of their skis. Even more startling is the human structure they've left behind. It's the only thing visible for miles and the first of their lifelines into the Antarctic interior.

The *Fram*'s gone by the time the depot party arrives back. The news makes for a subdued homecoming. They'd covered a distance of over 60 kilometres on the last day to be sure of seeing the ship and her crew off.

Amundsen takes a stroll out on the lonely edge of the Bay of Whales. A few dogs trail behind him, evidently bored to be home after the excitement of the depot journey. They give a start whenever Helmer discharges his shotgun. He's down by the water's edge hunting skua gulls. The seabirds have become a favourite dish, roasted and served with a dollop of Lindstrøm's cloudberry conserve. Helmer joins Amundsen at the spot of churned-up and dirty snow where the *Fram* was moored. It's a melancholy sight, a reminder of their isolation and the need to rely on each other.

'Did you see our little boat?' Helmer's question catches Amundsen temporarily off-guard. 'The lifeboat Captain Nilsen has left us.'

Amundsen nods. The top of its mast is just visible from the hut.

'Funny that Nilsen was so worried our camp might float out to sea.' Helmer stamps his feet. 'Feels quite solid underfoot to me.'

'Maybe Nilsen is worried about not making it back here. Sailing around the Horn to Buenos Aires. Facing off gales and mountainous seas with only nine crewmen.'

'Makes what we're planning look rather pleasant,' Helmer says with conviction.

Amundsen mutters something inaudible. He stares out at the dense heave of the Ross Sea. 'I do hope he can raise some funds in Buenos Aires.'

Helmer seeks to make eye contact. 'To hire some fresh hands, you mean?'

Amundsen offers a false laugh. 'No, so he can re-provision the ship and come back for us. Nilsen has nothing left in his coffers.'

Helmer smiles at the joke. '*Nothing?*'

'I mean — nothing.' Amundsen's eyes widen. 'Not a penny. No money for repairs, no money for fuel, for food or drink or tobacco or even postage stamps. He certainly doesn't have any money to pay the crew.'

'Sounds familiar,' huffs Helmer, referring to the dire financial fortunes of their Northwest Passage expedition, when they'd had to set sail under the cover of darkness to escape their Norwegian creditors. It had all worked out in the end though.

'You're right, Helmer!' Amundsen laughs heartily. 'It's nothing we haven't seen already!'

CHAPTER TWENTY

Barely a day passes and the men are already thrown into preparations for the second depot journey. Amundsen paces back and forth, consumed by the question of weight. He knows significant reductions are possible and devotes all his energy to imagining the ways this can be achieved. If they can pack provisions more efficiently, that will reduce the burden on the dogs. With lighter loads the sledges themselves could be downsized. The heavy rigid sledges they've brought from Norway are simply not necessary. What they need are light, flexible sledges like the ones used by the Netsilik. Stubberud could easily strip them back. In pondering the question of weight, it has occurred to the chief that another way to lessen their load is to leave men behind. Fewer men require fewer provisions. But the question of which men to take and which men to leave is a tricky one. Helmer is his right-hand man. Sverre is highly experienced with dogs. Bjaaland's the champion on skis, and fast. Prestrud and Oscar are green but diligent workers. Stubberud's handyman skills could be lifesaving on the trail. And Johansen has survival knowledge the others lack. Thank goodness Fatty is not built for sledging. That's one man he can leave out. Perhaps by the end of winter, he'll have a firmer view.

'I really, really hate these boots,' Prestrud says, slicing away the canvas from the sole with a heavy pair of scissors. On his face is a look of pure glee. 'I feel like a surgeon.'

'I prefer executioner,' chuckles Helmer. He's removed the entire top of his boot and dangles its collapsed form over the table in ghoulish delight. 'It looks quite harmless now, doesn't it? No longer capable of inflicting pain and sorrow on the poor unsuspecting foot.'

There's a hum of approval around the table. Everybody is caught up in their own form of disassembling and re-stitching of ski boots. It's become the evening's entertainment after supper. Oscar has proven particularly adept at shaving away layers of the sole to make it more pliable while still retaining enough stiffness to attach correctly to the ski bindings. Impressed at the younger man's handiwork, Amundsen has handed over his boots and simply requested that Oscar 'make them better'. There appears to be no right or wrong way of improving them. Each man has been given the responsibility of correcting the limitations of his own kit. Already hats have been redesigned and while all sorts of strange inventions have emerged from the process, nobody laughs at the creations taking shape. Johansen has sacrificed his most prized Icelandic wool sweater. What was once a sleeve is now peculiar headgear, a hood of sorts with eye sockets that makes him look part criminal, part sideshow spectacle.

'You may laugh now,' he says wearily to the men assembled at the table. 'But when I've got a nose and you have nothing but a frostbitten stub on your faces, it might just be me sniggering at you.'

Seven sledges set out on the morning of 22 February. Eight men head away on skis. Prestrud is once again the frontrunner but this time the lieutenant wears boots that no longer pinch his feet when worn with four pairs of socks and an insulating layer of dried sennegrass. The commotion that is inevitable when forty-two impatient dogs set off at a gallop can still be heard when the teams disappear over the ridge and onto the Great Ice Barrier. But the continent swallows the sound soon enough into its vast empty belly.

Lindstrøm yawns, knocks the snow off his reindeer kamiks and steps back into the warmth of the Framheim hut. It could be a month before they return. Lindstrøm conjures up an image of what his daily life will look like. More organising. The entry into the hut is now enclosed and the men have dug out a 1.5-metre-wide passageway around the perimeter. Quite a bit of snow has accumulated over the first weeks and by extending the roof of the hut over the passageway all the way down to the ground, the men have created an ample storage space for all Lindstrøm's provisions, with shelves cut into the snow to store fresh meat, and a quarry of sorts where the cook can excavate as much clean snow as he needs for his kitchen. Clean snow has become a precious resource with so many dogs on the loose. Yellow snow, brown snow – there's certainly plenty of that to go around.

'Sweet solitude,' Lindstrøm sighs, returning to the chaos left in the wake of the men's departure. Of course he's not completely alone and this time will be far from relaxing – seventy dogs that require his attention will make sure of that.

CHAPTER TWENTY-ONE

Only a week has passed but their old tracks have disappeared. Nevertheless, Prestrud manages to spot the first flag at the 10-kilometre mark. Shortly after he comes across the first of the dried-fish markers. His gaze latches to the dark shape in his otherwise monotonous field of vision. He grabs and throws the fish to one side for Helmer to stash on the sledge before any of the dogs can snap it up – it'll be needed to feed them later that afternoon.

The snow is deep and porridge-like. 'Corn snow', according to Amundsen. It's heavy, sweaty work to break through it hour after hour, with the granular texture offering a gluey resistance to their skis and sledge runners. Helmer shouts at Prestrud to alter his course this way or that. The lieutenant's mood darkens. By the third day Prestrud is spoiling for a fight. Not only must he cut a trail for everyone but at the end of the day he's expected to cook too. Throughout the day his rage builds, his ill humour stoked by a crippling gale from the south-east that buffets his body and savages his face with a barrage of tiny ice particles. The dried fish have disappeared from view, obscured by the wind that churns the surface into a white slurry and turns everything to a blur. The shouting from behind grows in intensity.

'Left, I said!'

This time there are four tents, with cooking taking place in two. Stubberud has dinner well underway in his tent before Prestrud can even make a start on his preparations. He is freezing cold but has nothing to cook and nowhere to cook it. He shelters in the lee of one of the other tents while he waits for Johansen to arrive with the stove and their tent. His muttering is almost comical.

'Don't be a martyr. Come in,' yells Stubberud through the canvas.

'I'll just get my boots off and he'll arrive,' Prestrud yells back. 'He does it on purpose, I swear! Making me wait every bloody time.'

'His dogs are useless, that's why he's last,' Oscar says as he slips into the tent, pleased to have discharged all his duties for the day.

Johansen's outline materialises from the white whirl of windblown snow, his snow hood encased in a layer of ice. His dogs fall out of rhythm with each other as they sense an end to their toil. Johansen tosses his whip onto the sledge. Its shaft is broken in two places. Overuse is the cause. He's going to have to repair it tonight if he's to get these miserable curs going in the morning.

Prestrud strides towards him, lips tight. 'Where have you been?' he demands.

Johansen unstraps his skis. 'Antarctica. You?'

'I've been waiting an hour in this wind. Everybody else is warm, eating their supper. I can't do a thing until you arrive with our tent and the stove.'

Johansen gestures at his dogs, their paws matted with blood. 'What do you make of that? Sunday picnic? You go merrily on your way, out in front.' Johansen flails his hands in a mocking dance. 'Do you have any idea what it takes to keep these creatures going? Here you are, impatient and bad-tempered. You're not the only one with chores at the end of a long day. I've got to feed my dogs, unload the sledges, sort the harnesses.' Johansen rips off his gloves to retrieve the cooking equipment. He shoves it at Prestrud's belly and begins the task of uncoupling his dogs from the traces, his fingers increasingly clumsy as the freezing air begins to sink its teeth into his exposed flesh.

There's little conversation that evening in their cramped two-man tent even with Amundsen and Sverre joining them for the meal. Each man is sucking down his pemmican with grim focus.

'These tents are not big enough,' Johansen observes between mouthfuls.

Amundsen eyes him over the rim of his bowl. He has little patience for grumbling. He's already heard more than enough from Prestrud. The men are all tired, brimming with petty complaints – they've all got something to gripe about. But Johansen is right. If they're to avoid conflict then they'd better rethink their sleeping arrangements.

CHAPTER TWENTY-TWO

Blood-caked fur as black as seaweed is impossible to ignore. Faint red prints on the snow are a common sight. The dogs whimper when they lick their paws. Helmer examines his dogs one at a time. 'For goodness sake,' he says. 'The snow crust is cutting them to ribbons.'

'Haven't had a chance to harden up yet,' says Sverre matter-of-factly.

Getting the dogs to their feet each morning with the temperature frequently nudging minus 30 is becoming increasingly difficult. Shouting gets a few dedicated individuals up but the vast majority register the human presence with a blink or two then curl even more tightly onto themselves to conceal their faces.

It's taken them the best part of a week to reach their depot at 80 degrees south. Everything is as they left it and surprisingly little snow has gathered around the depot mound itself. They add 400 kilos of dog pemmican, 25 kilos of seal steaks, 40 kilos of fat and 13 kilos of margarine. Prestrud takes delight in informing Amundsen that he has completed a theodolite reading (something they were unable to do on the previous journey due to faulty equipment) and determined the depot's position to be at 79 degrees, 59 minutes. It's astonishing how accurately they judged their position given the only available tools were the sledge-meter and dead reckoning. To be triple sure of returning to the correct spot, they decide to stake out twenty bamboo poles running east–west to the depot at half-kilometre intervals. Each flag is numbered one to ten relative to the depot, so even if they should miss their mark, there's a 5-kilometre safety buffer on either side that will alert them to any error in their instruments.

Beyond 80 degrees the temperature drops even further. The days are clear, the sun bright, but it is as if some pitiless god has banished all pleasure from the world. They might as well be staring at a painting of the sun, for all the warmth they gain from its intense light.

Amundsen's feet are wet. There's nothing he can do to keep them dry in his boots. Each evening he dries his multiple pairs of woollen socks in the radiant heat of the Primus and spreads the sennegrass that has been insulating his soles. The dampness only returns the next day, an unwelcome but nonetheless familiar travelling companion.

'The Netsilik wear no socks at all, they just use grass,' he says. 'Here I am fussing with my woollens.'

Sverre grunts and burrows deeper into his sleeping bag, a clear sign that he's not interested in a discussion about the merits of wool socks or sennegrass, or any footwear in fact. His breath is needed for more pressing tasks, like raising the temperature in his sleeping bag. All too soon, it will be time to leave the relative warmth and face the rime frost that will cover every surface in the tent by morning.

Amundsen winces. Sitting is excruciating, and the act of skiing a source of intense discomfort. It's the diet, of course. Sledging rations. Are others suffering too? Surely somebody would have mentioned their rear end by now – either in earnest or in jest. No doubt his tent mate would have complained bitterly about any such inconvenience. Then again, haemorrhoids are not really the grandest topic of conversation at mealtimes.

His thoughts turn to the dogs. Several of the men had difficulty getting their teams to go forward. Even with half a kilo of dog pemmican a day, they're underfed and losing condition as the days go by. His own team is flagging, their gait less energetic, more untidy. One in particular, Odin, has developed a nasty sore under his shoulder where the harness has rubbed off both fur and skin. He's noted it in his sledging diary along with the temperature and the day's distance – a respectable 16 kilometres. The going has been mostly good. They're climbing slightly now as they approach their goal. Tomorrow won't be such a long day. They'll get there without much effort, erect the depot, allow the dogs a day's rest. Only Amundsen, Johansen, Oscar, Prestrud and Helmer will carry on to 82 and 83 degrees, where they'll leave another two caches of supplies. Bjaaland, Stubberud and Sverre will return to Framheim, and they'll need to take Odin with them, strapped to the empty sledge like cargo. Carrying on with a team of five dogs in minus 40 degrees will test Amundsen's ability as a sledge driver. Undoubtedly a fair amount of the whip will be required to convince the remaining dogs of his skill. Even his beloved Three Musketeers are losing heart.

Stubberud is happy enough when Amundsen tells him to head home. The carpenter is battle-weary and finding the cold a drain on his mental resources. The days of blankness set him thinking of home, almost hallucinating the concentrated green borders of the fjords. The thermometer reads minus 45 degrees – the coldest day yet.

Having finished marking out the depot east to west with sections of broken-up crate, he pulls his hood up and gives a shout to set his dogs in motion. Bjaaland will follow and Sverre will bring up the rear, keeping a close eye on the dogs and men. The poor state of the dogs strikes him as more serious than anyone cares to admit.

'Think you'll make it? All the way to 83 degrees?' Sverre goads Helmer. Rivalry often marks their exchanges. 'It's pretty cold.'

'Sure.' Helmer secures two lashings across Odin's crabbed form, taking care not to draw them too tightly against the dog's back.

Sverre asks, 'How many dogs do you think you'll lose?' It's gentle prodding but prodding nonetheless.

'I don't plan on losing any,' Helmer says, ruffling Odin's furry head. 'Just make sure you don't.'

CHAPTER TWENTY-THREE

The politely undulating ground has given way to peculiar lumpen formations, erupting from the surface like hay stacks. Prestrud picks a line and tries to keep to it, but in this field of strange features, deviations are inevitable. So too the loud criticisms from Helmer whenever he thinks the forerunner's deviations are too aggressive. For this reason Prestrud assumes the shouting is directed at him. It's not. The shouting is because Helmer's three leading dogs have disappeared. There one moment, gone the next.

Helmer hefts the sledge over onto its side to keep it from slipping further, should the other dogs be dragged into the crevasse by the weight of their colleagues. The barking of the remaining dogs sends spikes of sound into the still air; lower howls issue from below the snow. Helmer plants his skis over the ragged fissure and peers down. Dangling in their harnesses, the dogs are clearly distressed, nipping and growling at each other in confusion while they knock and jostle against slick ice walls.

'It's reasonably narrow, but deep,' he says when Amundsen pulls level with his team.

Amundsen scans the surroundings. They'd all remarked on the change in the landscape over the last day or two. He sees it now for what it is: a clear indication of danger lurking below. Prestrud must have passed right over the hazard, his long skis distributing enough of his weight that the snow bridge below him did not collapse.

Oscar arrives on the scene, then Johansen, who settles his team some way back and skis towards the assembled party. 'They alive?'

Helmer nods. 'We'll need to be careful pulling them back up though. They could easily slip their harnesses and I can't see the bottom.'

'Rotten surface,' Johansen says, pointing out the hummocks. 'We're clearly in a crevasse field. Someone should've told Prestrud.'

'Yes, yes,' Amundsen nods impatiently. 'Fine to say that now.'

One by one the dogs are pulled to the surface. First Helge, then Mylius, then Ring. They're not heavy, but each dog wriggles and bucks as it tries to get free, unwittingly endangering its safe passage to the surface. None of them show any signs of injury but in manhandling them, Helmer gets a fresh appreciation of their woeful skin-and-bone condition under the deceptive volume of fur. Again Sverre's words rise to confront him. *How many dogs do you think you'll lose?*

'Can they still pull?' asks Amundsen.

'For now,' Helmer says cautiously, checking their legs.

'My team's almost completely . . .' Johansen starts to speak.

'Yes, yes, I know. Mine too,' Amundsen snaps in irritation. The emaciated dogs weigh heavy on his conscience. With the intense cold pressing in, it's hard to think straight. Then there's the bad surface, his damp feet, the constant, throbbing pain of his haemorrhoids – all of it has conspired against his plans to reach 83 degrees.

Amundsen takes a deep breath before giving his verdict. 'Let's continue to 82. We'll leave everything there and turn back. I think it best.'

They face a terrible battle. Another two days of wind and drift, overcast skies and, now they've passed through the hummocks, hauntingly empty vistas. Cracking the whip has little effect. The dogs bow their heads under its savage sting but have nothing more to give their masters, no fire in their stride or vigour in their shoulders. Often the men themselves must push the sledges from behind to deliver momentum to the exhausted cavalcade. Onward they crawl, amid shouts, howling and the dry shriek of the wind.

Two weeks they've been out in the wild. March 8 marks the end of their southward journey. It's a remarkable achievement, bringing over half a tonne of supplies 260 kilometres closer to the pole. It will take them a few hours to organise the depot at 82 degrees south, which consists mainly of dog pemmican. The weather is clear and calm. They pitch their tents and enjoy a day of rest, satisfied that they can finally head home.

By the time they're ready to leave the temperature has plunged to minus 32 degrees and the wind has picked up. Long strips of dark blue fabric flap in angry salute atop Amundsen's sledge, which has been positioned on its end to further accentuate the location of their precious supplies. The 12-foot depot mound signals victory of a sort, but not one that anyone feels inclined to celebrate. Several of the dogs must be lifted to their feet and warmth massaged into their frozen limbs before they can even stand on their own. Resentful of the brutality that was required to get the dogs this far, each of the men shudders at the dark effort of returning to Framheim. The homeward journey is sure to exact a heavy toll.

Two days later the temperature hovers around minus 39 degrees. A storm bursts in from the south-east. Their best course of action will be to take shelter. The wind howls its demonic chorus. It claws at the tents for two long days, gnawing at the ropes and straining the thin fabric protecting the men from the full fury of the storm. When the worst is over and the four men emerge, the scene outside is one of chaos.

'Where are the harnesses?'

'Where are the ski bindings?'

Johansen picks up what remains of his whip. The leather sheath has been stripped. Teeth marks score deep in the wooden handle. 'They've eaten the lot.'

Helmer swears. After a moment's reflection he says, 'I've got spare leather straps. That's the bindings at least. We'll have to use rope for harnesses.'

Johansen picks up a tent pole and whips it savagely through the air. 'This'll have to do.'

'We're short a few dogs.' Oscar looks about in confusion.

'Over there,' Helmer gestures casually to where the snow is piled high against one of the sledges.

The dogs are indeed buried beneath. *Are they dead?* Oscar unearths first one, then another and another, and gets them moving. But Thor, one of Amundsen's dogs, cannot be coaxed to his feet. Whining when touched, the animal is obviously gravely ill.

'Sorry, my friend,' Amundsen says with genuine emotion.

Oscar turns away just in time. He does not care to see the swift blow of the axe.

Thor's lifeless body is tossed onto the sledge to be divided up at the next camp to feed his colleagues. Amundsen's four remaining dogs have been shared between Oscar and Helmer's teams but are not capable of much pulling. Jens, one of the Three Musketeers, is too weak to even walk. He is loaded together with the sleeping bags and tents and given a free ride for as long as he survives. The sledges, empty of provisions now, still represent an excessive burden for the compromised dog teams; there'll be no hitching a ride like last time.

It's a despicable job cutting up dogs that are no longer good for anything other than their meat. They must all take turns, even soft-hearted Oscar, who retches repeatedly while Amundsen offers advice.

'I see why Thor was in such pain.' Amundsen points to the abscess filling the dog's entire chest cavity. 'It's been growing there a while, by the looks. Amazing that he had it in him to set out from Framheim, let alone get this far.'

Oscar presses his forearm to his nose to try and block the smell. 'What shall I do?'

Amundsen shakes his head. 'Bury it. The meat's spoiled.'

In the night there is a fearsome racket. Several of the dogs have dug up Thor's diseased carcass and are ripping into it with such frenzy that nobody can tear them from the foul feast. Most of the others, huddled and freezing like so many tightly bound knots in the snow, neither register the commotion nor display much sign of life. Johansen, swiping his tent pole back and forth with terrible menace, manages to chase the dogs a safe distance from the action so Oscar can once again bury the remains, this time much deeper in the snow. Nobody gets much sleep after that and an early start seems the only sensible option.

For several days in a row, the men manage to cover a distance of more than 20 kilometres a day. The remaining dogs have finally fallen into a rhythm. Perhaps it's because the weather is warmer; perhaps they simply sense their journey's end is ever nearer. Johansen's team in particular seem to have come into their own. For so long the slowest, most disobedient dogs, they now beat a steady trail homeward.

'Why are you stopping?' asks Amundsen, sliding to a halt beside Oscar.

'It's Lurven,' Oscar says, removing his skis and kneeling in the snow. 'He howled then just sat down.' The other dogs crowd around. Oscar bats their curious snouts away so he can get closer to Lurven, his leader, his best puller, in many ways his teacher.

Amundsen peers down at the animal. 'He's dead.'

'Can't be. He was pulling just a second ago.'

'Well, he's stopped breathing.'

'No.'

'He's dead, Oscar.' Amundsen sets to unbuckling the dog's harness, a gesture that confuses the other dogs into thinking the day's work is at an end.

'My best dog.' Oscar feels culpable. How did he not spot the dog's fatal decline? 'My best dog, worked to death.'

'Forget the eulogy,' says Amundsen briskly as he hefts the dead dog onto the sledge. 'Let's go.' Oscar just stares at the animal, uncomprehending.

'Come on,' encourages Amundsen. 'The others are getting away on us.'

Oscar knocks the snow from his boots and fastens his ski straps. He feels like vomiting.

That evening, Lurven's scrawny body is chopped up and fed to his ravenous companions. This time, Johansen does the job.

CHAPTER TWENTY-FOUR

Sweat-soaked socks loop over the backs of chairs; damp fur clothing hangs heavy from the ceiling. Seal meat spits violently in the frying pan, adding a gauzy haze to the already humid space. The dense meaty aroma sends saliva glands into overdrive. The men fidget and squirm in anticipation. Nobody can imagine anything more satisfying than the first bite of the seared black flesh. Lindstrøm is overjoyed.

'Eat up, lads. Plenty more where that came from.'

During their absence, Lindstrøm has piled snow around the external walls of their dwelling to keep it warm and snug over the winter months. It represents a monumental physical effort. Now with his eight colleagues around the dining table, Lindstrøm is content to return to the kitchen and leave any shovelling for the others.

'Eating a meal at a table,' sighs Oscar. 'What luxury.'

'Eating a meal that's actually hot – now that's luxury,' Johansen says sarcastically. He's still grumbling about having to carry his meals from the cooking tent out into the cold then back into his own tent. 'I know we're saving on weight by only having one cooker, but it's not practical and it's certainly not fair on those of us who have to eat lukewarm food day after—'

Amundsen braces himself for the torture of sitting down on his crippled behind. He expects to have a full debrief on all aspects of their latest depot journey, but he'd like to enjoy his first meal back at Framheim in peace before launching into detail. 'Okay, I think we all agree that the tent situation must be improved so everyone can enjoy the heat from the Primus, a hot meal and a chance to dry their socks and boots.'

Johansen murmurs his approval. The others look up from their meals but are too focused on enjoying real food after their month of pemmican to offer any opinion on expedition logistics.

'Only vegetables for me,' says Amundsen, refusing Lindstrøm's plate of seal steaks. The return journey has been pure agony, with his haemorrhoids worse than ever. Lindstrøm's plentiful preserves, tinned fruit and vegetables will aid his recovery, he hopes. Neither scurvy nor constipation exist in Lindstrøm's vocabulary.

The sounds of eating, cutlery clinking, enamel cups of coffee clanking, snorts, coughs and the occasional burp echo around the table.

'The dogs need hardening up,' says Amundsen suddenly.

'Two of mine died. Waited till we arrived back here,' says Stubberud. 'Can you believe that?'

'That's eight dogs we've lost during the depot-laying.'

Sverre looks up. 'Is that counting Odin? You know he didn't make it.'

Amundsen nods grimly.

'He was so weak, even a ride on the sledge wasn't . . .' Sverre's voice trails off. 'How on earth are they going to make it to the pole?'

'You mean how are *we* going to make it to the pole?' snorts Bjaaland.

Silence meets his comment. Voicing doubt is reckless in the presence of the chief.

'It's just the cold,' says Johansen. 'If we'd had reasonable temperatures they'd have come through fine.'

'I agree,' says Amundsen, pushing his plate away and resting his pale forearms on the table to relieve some of

Self-possessed and incisive, Roald Amundsen exudes the confidence and fearlessness of a true polar hero. At over 180 centimetres tall with piercing blue eyes, he is the very embodiment of the Viking spirit.

The care of dogs provides a welcome diversion during the long and often monotonous sea voyage from Norway to the Bay of Whales. Here Captain Thorvald Nilsen feeds a puppy while its mother watches on.

Aboard the *Fram*. Top row from left: Sverre Hassel (1st), Olav Bjaaland (4th), Oscar Wisting (8th); Middle from left: Hjalmar Johansen, Kristian Prestrud, Roald Amundsen, Captain Nilsen, Lieutenant Gjertsen, Helmer Hansen; Front from left: Adolf Lindstrøm, Jørgen Stubberud.

Every man takes responsibility for fine-tuning his sledging outfit, headgear and goggles to suit his individual needs and preferences. The result is an impressive, if comical, array of improvements.

By autumn, Framheim has almost entirely disappeared under a deep layer of snow, which serves to insulate the hut from the severe Antarctic winter while providing the necessary conditions for an ambitious tunnelling operation.

Hauling heavily laden sledges over difficult terrain, the dogs sometimes need the encouragement of the whip. Keeping pace with the dogs, the skier steadies the load over uneven ground to lessen the possibility of capsizing.

Hjalmar Johansen warms his hands, taking a break from the packing of milk powder and other provisions into the newly honed sledging cases in the ice cave they've nicknamed the 'Crystal Palace'.

Olav Bjaaland poses for a photo in his reindeer sledging outfit and fur kamiks. In his hand he holds one of the dog harnesses. Fur clothing, while exceedingly warm, is prone to developing bare patches that must be mended – a useful pastime for long winter nights.

Expedition chef and the first person ever to sail around the Americas, Adolf Lindstrøm is shown here holding a plate of his famous pancakes, which sustained the morale of Amundsen and his crew throughout the first navigation of the Northwest Passage and for a year in Antarctica.

Roald Amundsen, Helmer Hansen, Sverre Hassel and Oscar Wisting share a solemn moment at the South Pole ahead of the perilous return journey. Thirty-four days later the tent and a random assortment of clothing and equipment will be discovered by Captain Scott and his four companions, signalling their defeat.

Oscar Wisting poses with his dogs at the South Pole. The Norwegians spend three days at the pole, using a range of instruments to fix their position and ensure beyond a doubt that they have reached 90 degrees south. However, the race is not over until the news reaches the world.

the pressure on his rear end. 'And food. They'll need more food.'

'More food means heavier sledges,' says Helmer in a dispirited tone. 'Heavier sledges means more food – it's a bloody joke.'

'Unless we lighten the sledges,' says Bjaaland, keen to make up for his earlier negativity. 'Stubberud and I could easily take to them with the plane, trim down the other components without weakening the structure. And the packing cases too could be shaved down to save on weight.' He turns to the carpenter. 'What do you think?'

'We got the tools,' Stubberud agrees.

'And a long winter ahead of us,' adds Bjaaland.

Amundsen purses his lips. 'Good. I think we could overhaul a lot of our equipment. But we'll still need more food.' He pauses in thought. 'One more depot trip. Just to 80 degrees. Before winter arrives properly. If we stockpile as much seal meat as we can there, then the dogs'll be in the best possible shape.'

A murmur of agreement swells from the table.

'You'll lead,' Amundsen says, pointing his chin in Johansen's direction. 'I'll wait this one out with Fatty.'

Amid the rowdy conversations that ensue, Johansen squeezes his nose between his thumb and forefinger to disguise his grin.

CHAPTER TWENTY-FIVE

What was once pristine white landscape around Framheim is a now a minefield of excrement. The dogs are on the prowl, all seventy of them. Big and small, they range about in twos and threes, nosing in drifts of snow for whatever remains of the seals that were butchered for meat. Nothing in the Norwegian camp escapes their interference. Boxes are over-turned. Ropes are gnawed at. The tents are layered with wild maps of yellow ice, the result of the dogs' never-ending quest to mark as much territory as possible while their comrades are away. Everywhere they go, they leave mess. Little can be done, as there's no longer any other reason to keep the dogs chained up. Lindstrøm stretches barbed wire around Framheim to keep them from clambering up the steadily accumulating snow and onto the roof while Amundsen builds a perimeter wall from blocks of snow to barricade the tent used to store precious meat supplies. But the dogs are persistent and have learnt that if they jump high enough they can steal into the store. Soon Amundsen is unfurling barbed wire as well.

With the exterior dog-proofed, Lindstrøm turns his attention to the hut's interior. It's in a filthy state. Nine men sleeping, eating, working and drying sodden clothing and footwear has made a mockery of the strict order he had established during their previous absence.

'Good grief,' he mumbles as he examines a box full of dirty, worn-out reindeer kamiks found lurking under a bunk. 'This place is a rat's nest.' He flings the box and its contents out through the open door of the hut. The kamiks scatter on the snow and are immediately snapped up by a pack of excited dogs. The trouble is there are too few to go around. Some dogs tear off with a prize in their jaws. The less fortunate follow in hot pursuit. A fight erupts over the remaining spoils but not one dog gets to enjoy a smelly bootie in its entirety. Within minutes, they're torn to shreds. Clumps of reindeer fur and clumps of dog fur litter the snow.

'We'll have to go through the same filthy stage when the others get back,' sighs Amundsen, hefting another pot of boiling water off the coal range and into the washing tub on the kitchen floor. 'We have to maintain order in here or we'll go mad. We'll kill each other.'

Amundsen heads outside and scans the surrounding area for snow that's clean enough to melt for cleaning. When he returns, Lindstrøm is furiously wiping down the walls. 'Fat,' he says by way of explanation, 'from all the frying.'

The pot of snow is again on the heat. Another one and the washing tub will be sufficiently full for his purpose. Amundsen dips a cloth in the hot water and joins Lindstrøm at his task.

'A means of escape, that's what each man needs. Somewhere to get away from others,' Lindstrøm says. 'Do you remember on the *Gjøa*, when we were caught in the ice over winter? That was a bloody small boat. It didn't take long for us to figure out it was better to learn how to make an igloo from the Netsilik and get a bit of space from our shipmates. Pity they never gave us a moment's peace though – always visiting!' Lindstrøm laughs at the memory.

'Shall I suggest that then, Fatty? That we each construct an igloo to see out the winter?'

Lindstrøm groans. 'Oh no, we'd all go mad from loneliness.'

Amundsen smiles. He feels fortunate to have a man so good-natured, so positive in his outlook on his team once again. Just like the old days.

The cook continues his train of thought, 'It's almost as if we all need to head out to work in the morning and come back together in the evening to share a meal, play cards or listen to the gramophone. If we've all been busy during the day, we'd have something to talk about.'

'Yes, I see what you mean. There's certainly lots to do ahead of our polar journey. Problem is, it's winter. Working outside is just not possible.'

'Well, I've got my larder carved out of the snow beside the hut but I don't fancy sharing that space with the dust and muck of the carpenters or with the constant whirring of Oscar's sewing machine.' Lindstrøm straightens his jacket and takes a moment to admire the fresh appearance of the hut's degreased walls. 'Your water's boiling.'

'I'm going to close the door now,' says Amundsen. 'Any more cold air circulating in here and the water in my tin tub will freeze.'

'Can you spare some?' Lindstrøm asks as he watches the chief tip the last pot of steaming liquid into what has become an otherwise lukewarm tub. 'You won't need all of that to wash your clothes.'

Amundsen swirls his hand through the water. It's pleasingly hot, but given the chill still pervading the hut, he doesn't have long before it will start to cool to the point of unpleasantness. Deftly sliding out of his kamiks, he pulls his pants and woollen underwear off. He wrestles off his jacket, sweater, wool shirt and undershirt. His socks he leaves until last.

The washing tub's not big and the chief is a very tall man. The sight of Amundsen dipping his pale rear end into the water sets Lindstrøm giggling like a schoolboy.

Amundsen frowns comically. 'You did say you wanted to thoroughly clean everything in the hut.'

Lindstrøm hands the chief a cloth and some soap. Then, still chuckling, he grabs his hat and heads outside for a walk. Allowing a bit of privacy is the least he can do to ensure full enjoyment of this momentous event – Amundsen's first proper wash in seven months.

Chapter twenty-six

Fresh dogs, fat and keen, scamper forward towing their heavy loads over the uneven surface in a display of unbridled enthusiasm. They're a far cry from the dogs that returned from the last depot-laying journey, limping and harassed by the whip. It will take those dogs some weeks to regain their condition. This time a number of the older puppies have entered the fray, interspersed among the mature dogs so any youth and inexperience can be held in check.

Matching their momentum, Johansen skis in smooth, confident strides like an insect on the surface of a pond. He feels liberated. The alcohol abuse, his failed marriage, the children he hasn't seen in years – none of it weighs so heavy anymore. The only thing that counts is where he is now – the majesty of this boundless arena, welcoming him into its forgiving embrace. This is where he belongs. He will achieve greatness at the pole. He will be a national hero again. Redemption awaits!

You're the leader, that's what Amundsen said and everybody heard him say it. For the first time since setting sail aboard the *Fram*, Johansen has received official recognition of his polar credentials. After experiencing the fame associated with being Fridtjof Nansen's right-hand man, it's been a struggle reverting to being just one of the men, constantly deferring to Amundsen and his judgement when he has just as much to offer. And on board the *Fram*, taking orders from young officers who have not yet proven themselves. More than once, while scrubbing dog turds off the decking, he'd considered dousing Lieutenant Prestrud with a bucket of salt water.

The fog is sly in its approach. Nobody notices its slow strangulation of the sky. The brilliant blue becomes faded, then briefly grey before surrendering to an impenetrable dullness. The flat light is disorientating. The men continue regardless, but in a direction further west than anyone realises.

Johansen calls to Stubberud. 'Remember, one flag every kilometre.'

The carpenter signals he's understood. The flagpoles are taller than a man and are indispensable now that they're losing the light. Shorter days, dark nights, foul autumn weather. Disagreeable.

'There's nothing out here. No markers, no frozen fish,' says Helmer, pulling level with Johansen. 'Stubberud can forget about laying his flags. This is not our old route. We're lost.'

'We're not lost,' says Johansen, annoyed at Helmer's unhelpful comment, but he halts the team and hollers to Prestrud.

Prestrud is clear on their last known coordinates and he's thankful that it was not his navigating that led them astray. 'Do you want a compass heading?' he asks Johansen.

Johansen nods. 'And the sledge-meter. What distance have we covered, Oscar?'

'Last time I saw one of our old broken-up markers was about an hour ago,' offers Helmer.

Johansen tips back his head and squints into the glare. Flat light. There's no telling the position of the sun and therefore no possibility of taking angles with a sextant. But he continues to stare at the possibility of the sun's disc, using some mysterious past knowledge to determine their next course of action. 'By my reckoning we've travelled too far west. We need to carry on in a south-easterly direction to correct. We'll come across our old tracks or the markers soon enough.'

There's plenty of grumbling, and backchat that they'd never engage in with the chief. Two days into a route that they have already successfully navigated twice and they're lost. Still, it's nobody's fault. It's easy to veer off course with such poor visibility.

'Halt!' shouts Johansen, diving onto his sledge. Two dogs are already gone.

Helmer, Sverre and Stubberud bring their dogs to heel. Prestrud, Bjaaland and Oscar appear from the gloom, unsure what the commotion is all about.

Thankfully Johansen keeps his head. He inches forward on his skis and peers down the crevasse, assessing the situation. 'Damn it,' he hisses in exasperation. 'Both gone.'

Some way off Oscar hears a curious thud. Suddenly a gap stretches open behind him, unzipping the surface with one smooth stroke. Snow tumbles in like a waterfall. His eyes widen in horror.

Sverre shouts obscenities as another gap opens up under his sledge with a loud hollow boom.

'Crevasse field,' calls Johansen to the others. 'Nobody move.'

The dogs are working themselves into a frenzy on the spot. The tension, the uncertainty underfoot, the confused arrangement of the various teams – all of it puts them on edge.

Helmer asks, 'What now?'

Johansen has already freed up some alpine rope from his sledge. With grim focus he ties a series of knots at equal intervals along its length. 'You and Sverre. You're going to rope up. I need you to check to the east. Make sure you move in parallel. And keep the rope taut. The knots will stop the rope from cutting in too deeply if one of you falls.'

Picking a way forward, Helmer and Sverre determine a safe route and double back for the sledges. For hours they work in tandem, applying the method suggested by Johansen. The danger lies in the ground appearing solid. But all it takes is one man's misstep and large pieces of the surface fall away, revealing bottomless crevasses that would swallow not just dogs but men and sledges too. Progress is slow but Johansen refuses to take chances. Just as the light is fading, Johansen deems their location sufficiently safe to set up camp. It's a relief after spending the best part of a day on tenterhooks, barely daring to breathe lest it trigger the collapse of the delicate snow bridges underfoot.

They're trialling new, larger tents: two sewn together, thanks to Oscar's skill with the sewing machine. With four men in one and three in the other, there's ample room for undressing, preparing food, and drying clothing and footwear.

Johansen examines his fur clothing, how worn it has become in parts. The seat of his trousers is utterly bare, now a bald expanse of leather devoid of any insulation. No wonder his rear end is frozen solid. The others have similar complaints with the deteriorating state of their clothing. Looks like a whole winter of repairs.

'Not a bad test for the dog harnesses,' says Oscar, dishing up the pemmican stew.

Stubberud snorts. 'I'm not sure Johansen would agree. He's lost his two leading dogs.'

Johansen jerks his head in agreement.

Oscar continues, 'The fact that the dogs are each individually attached to the sledge is a great idea, isn't it? Being fanned out like that. If the dogs had been two by two in those Alaskan harnesses, Johansen would have lost all his dogs – and the sledge too, probably.'

'That Amundsen,' says Stubberud admiringly. 'He knows his stuff.'

'Sure does,' Oscar is quick to agree. 'Everything has a clear purpose.'

Well, it wasn't Amundsen who led you out of trouble today, was it, lads? Johansen thinks sourly. *And not a word of thanks or acknowledgement of my skill.* Without another word, he licks clean his bowl and places it beside him, ready for the morning meal. *Perhaps next time, I'll let them blunder their own way out of danger.*

APRIL 1895 – ARCTIC CIRCLE

Johansen's trousers are sodden, his boots waterlogged. He hauls himself back from the jagged edge where the ice has given way to rippling water. Fridtjof Nansen watches on. Neither man speaks. Words do nothing to lighten the gravity of their situation. They are far from land. How far, neither of them dares suggest. The sea ice is no longer sure underfoot. Great rents appear in its surface as wind and currents conspire, forming wide avenues of open sea that stretch for miles.

Johansen's wet trousers adhere to his skin. Within minutes the outer layer has frozen to a hard shell and his boots clench to his feet.

He wiggles his toes to establish a line of communication with his extremities. It's futile. His body will soon disavow all knowledge of these feet, so numb on the ends of his legs as to feel like they belong to somebody else.

'Shall we try that way?' he mumbles to Nansen.

Nansen signals his agreement. It's the same either way. Far from land, with dwindling food supplies and no idea of their precise location, the men hold it together with a grim determination that belies their wretched fate. It feels like the days never end. Trudging forth, his frozen lower half in denial, Johansen adds 'exposure' to his growing list of ways to die – by drowning, by starvation, by polar bear.

The dog that struggles to keep up is earmarked for supper. A bullet to the brain would be best but their rifle has other duties – hunting, protection against predators. Strangulation will have to do. The dog whines as the rope is wound around its neck. Positioned on either side of the timorous creature, the two men take up the slack. Pulling mightily on either end of the rope, Johansen and Nansen bellow in guttural distaste. It is a beastly task.

'I can't,' Johansen says finally, releasing the rope.

Without a word, Nansen reaches for a knife. Holding the dog's shoulders between his knees, he slits its throat. It's a messy business. The blood courses down his legs and over the snow. Johansen feels a pang of jealousy. Death appears as an easy end.

CHAPTER TWENTY-SEVEN

Lindstrøm sits bolt upright. His head slams into the empty bunk above. A howl explodes in the dark. Amundsen turns sleepily to assess the level of injury.

'You okay?'

'The travellers are coming home.'

Amundsen closes his eyes. 'You're having a dream, Fatty. Go back to sleep.'

'They'll be here today at noon.'

Amundsen grunts.

Lindstrøm rubs the top of his bald head. There's a small amount of blood where his scalp has been scraped.

He won't get back to sleep now. Instead he drops to the floor. Flicking on the lamp in the kitchen, he sees his lucky ladle has fallen from its hook on the wall. Lindstrøm cradles the utensil, his hand checking its rounded hemisphere for dents. Finding no damage, he places it back on the hook, his smile like that of a mother doting on a favourite child. *Thank you*, he mouths.

Signs and portents – they're as much part of Lindstrøm's charm as his cooking. Everyone takes his folk wisdom with a pinch of salt, but nobody dares challenge the cook on his predictions. More often than not, they prove correct.

The hut is pitch black but it's not the middle of the night – it's six-thirty. It won't get much brighter anyway. The days are so dull now that they must keep the lamps burning inside all day if they're to see what they're doing. Lindstrøm stacks logs in the stove, sloshes over a liberal dose of paraffin then touches a match to the wood. It flares extravagantly, illuminating the darkened kitchen in its fierce light. The fire roars in the chimney. He peers under the tea towel covering the bowl of pancake batter he mixed up the night before and readies his equipment. Lindstrøm's workspace has an odd appearance – half laboratory, half kitchen. Two mercury barometers, four aneroids for measuring air pressure, a barograph, thermograph and one thermometer occupy the corner furthest from the stove. Lindstrøm would eye the whole enterprise suspiciously if it hadn't been he himself who had set up the meteorological instruments. There's a corresponding meteorological station on the hill with all the outside equipment housed in a tidy whitewashed instrument box that Lindstrøm has constructed this week, complete with a handsome weathervane to show wind direction. He's very proud of it.

With the kettle heating on the stove the cook begins to grind the coffee. Round and round with the handle for ten minutes he works, his ruddy cheeks shaking with the effort. 'This coffee mill is not worth throwing to the pigs,' he mutters in frustration. 'Might as well chew the beans!'

It's only the two of them but the morning routine proceeds as if it were a full house. At twenty to eight Lindstrøm opens the door from the kitchen, unleashing the intense heat that has become almost unbearable in the enclosed space. It sweeps into the tight living quarters, which are kept purposefully cold for sleeping. Having lit the lamps he readies the table, making as much noise as possible: clanging the enamel plates and dropping spoons into coffee mugs from such a height it'd wake the dead. There's movement behind the dark red curtain drawn across Amundsen's bunk. If the others were home, there'd be swearing by now. Satisfied that his table-setting performance has had the appropriate effect, Lindstrøm returns to his frying pan, where he'll turn out pancakes with machine-like efficiency until the bowl is empty and the plates are stacked. There'll be much organising to do when the others return and a whole lot more cooking. The men's appetites will be insatiable, like greedy ogres in a fairytale. *Noon*, Lindstrøm nods with conviction.

'Morning Fatty,' says Amundsen, yawning. 'How's the weather?'

'Easterly breeze. Fog,' he says evenly despite not having set foot outside.

'Temperature?'

Lindstrøm screws up his face. 'Minus sixteen.'

'That's your guess?' Amundsen reaches for his notebook and writes it down.

It's a relatively new game, getting the men to guess the temperature each morning. It's an educated guess he's after, not a bold-faced fabrication like Lindstrøm's. At the end of the month the man closest to the actual mean temperature is awarded a cigar, a book, a very nice gold watch. Everyone's keen for the prize but the game serves another purpose. Every man is finely calibrating his senses, learning to read the environmental conditions and trust in his own judgement, which is a skill more highly prized than a cigar when one's equipment fails far from home.

The morning passes without much to differentiate it from all the other mornings the two men have shared since the others left. Breakfast is an unhurried affair with equal measures of conversation, reminiscences and companionable silence. Afterwards Amundsen unties the dogs and takes his customary morning stroll down onto the sea ice accompanied by any animals eager for a change of scene. There are fewer seals about. Soon there will be none at all to harangue. The dogs will have to find other pursuits. Icy seal carcasses may be tasty to gnaw on, but they don't put up enough of a fight for a dog keen on entertainment.

Amundsen barely registers the dogs and their antics. Thoughts occupy him. They steer him ever south, to Johansen and the others. They were due back on Saturday. It's now Tuesday. Will placing Johansen in charge change things? Group dynamic is vitally important. Especially ahead of the long winter confinement. Nine men all packed like sardines in the Framheim hut. Frustrations, petty annoyances, simmering conflict all have the potential to turn into something much larger, more destructive. And then there is Johansen, always ready to assert his position, hijack the conversation, trading endlessly on his friendship with Nansen as if it conferred special rights. In appointing Johansen leader of the last depot journey, Amundsen had hoped to defuse the tension. Has he instead set himself up for a power struggle?

Lindstrøm was wrong. The day is cold. Almost minus 30 degrees and it's blowing hard from the south. Days are shorter, the wind just a little sharper. Amundsen cuts short his walk and, wrestling the wind all the way, returns home to continue the repairs he started the previous day on his sleeping bag. Lindstrøm calls to him from the tent where the puppies have been housed.

'Any sign of Madeiro?' Amundsen asks.

'No. Must have fallen into a crevasse or tangled with the wrong bull seal. I don't want to tell Nilsen.'

There's a dog lying dead amid the gambolling youngsters. 'Our poor Angel of Death,' says Amundsen. The puppy had been christened thus aboard the *Fram*, so often had the poor wizened creature collapsed under its own weight. Against all odds, it had stayed alive and had even flourished. Until now.

'Look at *him*.' Lindstrøm gestures at another of the pups born on the *Fram*, the one christened 'Southern Cross'. His dark coat is a wretched sight – the fur is all but gone from his back. 'Probably got into a fight.'

Amundsen shakes his head. 'Looks like disease. Let's get him out of here before he infects the rest.'

It's a sorry business, dealing a death blow to a creature so new to the world. A mere skin disorder, no doubt, but one that could decimate their chances of setting off for the pole should enough of the dogs become infected. One thing a sledge dog in Antarctica needs is its thick winter coat.

When Amundsen returns from burying the two dead dogs, Lindstrøm is poised by the door to the hut with a look of mild satisfaction. According to their well-established routine, he should be in the kitchen preparing lunch. It is noon, after all.

'Look, Chief,' he says, pointing to dark specks peppering the horizon. 'I was right. They're home and not a moment too soon.'

CHAPTER TWENTY-EIGHT

Amundsen is wary of winter. Not the snow and ice, the all-pervading cold and hurtling winds – he can plan for those. It's the darkness he's afraid of. Unremitting, oppressive, the Antarctic winter saps mental strength. Steady, regular work, that's what each man needs – a purpose. Not useless work that will bore a man to tears or create feelings of resentment.

Bjaaland has been set the task of reworking the sledges. They need to be light, to be flexible, to be fast. He's already worked them over once but greater improvements are possible. Stubberud seems convinced he can reduce the weight of the sledging cases too, the boxes that carry their supplies. It should be possible to lose 3 kilos at least. Laborious as it is to shave off layer after layer of wood with a handheld planer, Stubberud knows it's all for a worthwhile cause. In the end he opts to use an axe to slice into the sides.

Once the boxes have been pared back sufficiently, Johansen will pack them even tighter with sledging provisions ready for their spring departure to the pole. His job's going to be even more tedious. Pemmican, milk powder, biscuits, chocolate – everything must be weighed, measured, counted. Twice or even three times. Patience and accuracy is needed when counting out thousands of biscuits. There will be no room for mistakes when the chief cracks open the biscuit tin out on the Great Ice Barrier.

Oscar will spend the best part of winter in front of his sewing machine, making repairs and adjustments to clothing, equipment and footwear, and enlarging the remaining tents. They all agree that the white tent fabric can be improved upon by using the only dye they have to hand – India ink. The darker shade of blue will be more restful to the eyes, easier to spot against their white surroundings and should absorb the feeble warmth of the sun more readily. Another issue they're keen to rectify is the incessant build-up of ice on the outside of the tents, which adds significant weight to the sledges. A fly sheet's the answer. Oscar is set to make a couple from the red curtains he's snaffled from each man's bunk.

'Less privacy, perhaps,' says Oscar resignedly. It scarcely matters. Whatever inhibitions they once harboured have been well and truly lost in such close quarters.

Prestrud has more than enough astronomical calculations to keep him busy all winter. Nobody would want his job, poor blighter. In time he'll teach them all the fundamentals of navigation, if only for safety's sake, but for now the men are happy to leave the lieutenant to pore over those deadly columns of figures in the lamplight day after day.

And where does shovelling snow fit into Amundsen's new order, in which every man needs a worthwhile occupation? Shovelling snow in this place is a bit like sweeping back the tide – pointless. Left to accumulate around the hut, the snow is like a slowly rising dough covering first the windows, then the walls and finally the roof. The front door is well below the new ground level. In fact their new entrance is a trapdoor in the snow opening to some rough-hewn stairs that descend to the front porch. The chimney cap with its drifting smoke is the only outward sign of human habitation. And that is how it should be – the hut is as snug as a burrow, protected from extreme weather and insulated from the deep freeze of Antarctica's coldest, darkest months.

The only issue remains the fuel. Ready access to fuel is vital for survival. Cooking, melting snow for water and heating the hut all require coal, wood or oil, which for safety's sake have been stored in a fuel cache a short distance from the hut. The oil drums now lie under a metre or more of snow, which hardens by the day as the rolling procession of storms dump yet more snow on top. Clearing this snow is indeed useful work. To neglect this shovelling would mean giving in to dehydration, hypothermia and starvation. Just because it's life-saving doesn't mean it's any less energy-sapping, and unfortunately Sverre must shoulder his responsibility as fuel master. He stands in the half-light with his shovel, contemplating the enormity of his task.

'Where's Sverre?' asks Oscar as the men sit down at lunchtime.

'Didn't you go out to fetch him?' Amundsen asks Stubberud.

The carpenter blinks. 'He wasn't out there. I thought he might have gone to relieve himself. And I'm not one for harassing a man with pressing business.'

The others laugh at the mere thought of privacy.

'It's snowing hard. Better nip out and check,' Amundsen nods at Stubberud, who eases himself up from the table with exaggerated reluctance. Fur clothing, balaclava, reindeer mitts, socks and fur kamiks – a right fuss – as if there was any such thing as 'nipping out' to check.

He's gone ten minutes or more. The others are eating, chatting, half-expecting two white figures to reappear at the door. 'Two of them missing now,' says Lindstrøm between bites.

Pushing his plate away, Bjaaland stands. 'I'll go.' The others shift their seats closer to the table, allowing him to squeeze past and grab his hat and outdoor clothes from his allotted pegs at the end of the bunks. A wall of cold air enters the hut as he bustles outside to investigate. Unsurprisingly, he too fails to return.

Helmer doesn't wait for his coffee. He's away out the door as soon as lunch is over, trading the peaceful digestion of his midday meal for the intensifying mystery of what is now three missing men. It doesn't take long for the others to take the bait. Amundsen and Prestrud kit up and head out, as do Oscar and Johansen. Lindstrøm is the last to emerge, reluctant to leave the warmth of the hut but not wanting to be the only man missing out on any unfolding drama.

Bracing themselves against the wind, the group gathers in the dizzying whirl of snow; some crouch, some bend double. Stubberud is moving about on his hands and knees. Sverre's there too, but only his head is visible. He's been far too busy to stop for lunch. The grotto he's carved out for himself allows easy access to the barrels of petroleum with the benefit of being out of the howling wind.

'We better arch the entrance. You don't want a cave-in,' says Stubberud.

They've all got suggestions. 'Extend a tunnel this way and you'll be linked to the house.'

'A bit further and the wood and coal tent will be accessible. You could tunnel up from below.'

'Imagine if we could dig a tunnel from the house to the toilet. Handy when you're in a hurry.'

'Indoor plumbing!'

'Well, almost.'

They all laugh at the novelty of it. Amundsen's thinking of all the other possibilities presented by this new approach to working with nature rather than against her. An underground carpenter's workshop. A sewing room for Oscar where he can spread out his tents. Helmer will need somewhere to load the sledges under cover so the hide lashings don't freeze.

'I could pack the provisions properly without snow blowing through everything,' says Johansen.

It appears they've inadvertently created another wintertime pursuit to keep themselves busy for a month or more.

Lindstrøm harrumphs. He'll leave them to their alfresco brainstorming session. *Just got home and they'll be leaving again now,* he thinks miserably. He can see tunnelling fever has taken hold.

CHAPTER TWENTY-NINE

Johansen's fingers burn. He rubs his hands vigorously and blows warmth between his palms. The action doesn't relieve the pain. Reluctantly he slips his hands into the pockets of his reindeer-skin trousers and wonders what task he can attend to while he waits for feeling to return to his icy digits. The little lamp on the table throws his shadow against the sparkling white walls of the cave. It lends far more light than its feeble flame would suggest, thanks to the wonderful reflective qualities of ice. If only it would lend a little warmth. It's got to be minus 20 at least, thinks Johansen, stamping his feet.

The 1321 cans of pemmican are round. Packing the pemmican into Stubberud's newly engineered crates creates a lot of empty space. He's pleased with his idea of packing little bags of milk powder 300 grams apiece between the rounds of pemmican, long white sausages tied with string to fill the voids. Fantastic idea, Amundsen conceded. It's just a pity Johansen's fantastic idea requires so much bare-fingered handling in the sharp cold of his 'Crystal Palace'.

His work space is stacked to the ceiling with sledging provisions to pack. Now he just needs to find space for 100 kilos of chocolate. Everything must be entered into the provision booklets that each man will carry on the polar journey. A main book will be looked after by the two tent leaders, marking off everything that is consumed to ensure an accurate assessment of all remaining supplies.

It's taken them a month, but their enthusiastic tunnelling efforts have resulted in an ingenious underground complex of interconnected workspaces. Even a sauna and toilet have been carved into the winter-hardened snow. Every morning the men get up, go outside for a minute or two to assess the temperature, eat breakfast and then head off to work, each occupied by a range of activities that will ultimately contribute to the success of their springtime push south. There's still so much to do before the official departure date – 1 November – and everybody enjoys reuniting at mealtimes and recounting their day's achievements under a cloud of tobacco smoke. They are working as one, united in a single purpose.

Hunched over and with his hands enjoying the warmth of the furry pockets, Johansen goes over again and again the amount of food he needs to pack. Making modifications wherever he can, Johansen knows the provisions must fit in twenty-eight crates, four per sledge. Not a millimetre of space can be wasted. Amundsen's calculations are precise – he's spent months working out how many calories each man will consume and what combination of foods will serve them best, right down to the 25 kilos of fresh meat that each dog carries under its shaggy winter coat. Pemmican packs a punch in terms of the energy it provides but it also weighs a tonne. Biscuits are lightweight but also light on nutritional value. They certainly don't offer the same warming effect as a pemmican stew. As always, it's a trade-off.

Johansen whistles as he slips down the narrow tunnel and into Bjaaland's woodworking realm. It's not a good idea to surprise a man at work with sharp tools. 'Permission to enter, champ,' he says by way of greeting.

Bjaaland looks up from the sledge runner he's planing down to a smooth surface. He smiles.

Johansen nods at the piles of wood shavings on the floor. 'We're all fixated on the same thing, I see. Weight.'

Bjaaland gives a knowing grunt. 'It's taken us this long to finish one sledge. We took it apart, shaved every single piece of it back to the minimum and lashed it together again. Our 74-kilo monster now weighs only 21 kilos. Not bad, eh?'

'And it's strong enough? My provisions are pretty heavy.' Johansen narrows his eyes. 'I've got 300 kilos on every sledge. Then there's 75 kilos of equipment on top of that.'

'Should be okay.' Bjaaland steps back and admires his handiwork. 'Wish I could say as much for my hand plane. The way I'm sharpening the blade every few hours, I'm afraid it's not going to survive this little holiday in Antarctica.'

'I'm freezing,' says Johansen suddenly. 'All the standing in one place. At least your work's more physical – keeps your blood pumping.'

'Oscar's set up a Primus in his sewing nook.'

'Not a bad idea, I might do the same.'

'Good luck squeezing the paraffin out of Sverre. He sits on his fuel supplies like a goose guarding its eggs.'

They laugh about that. If only Sverre knew how profligate Lindstrøm had become with his use of paraffin in the kitchen, spraying it around to get the morning fires roaring. He already calls the cook 'the woodswallower', such is his insatiable appetite for firewood.

'Seen the chief?' asks Johansen.

'Working on the new whips with Sverre.'

The whips. They need strengthening, that's for sure – the depot-laying journeys were proof of that. It's the handles that snap in situations of overuse. Generally speaking, the crack of the whip combined with the mild sting of the popper nipping at the dogs is enough to keep them motivated. But every so often a troublemaker is intent on spoiling the show. Picking fights on the go is the usual offence. For obvious reasons these individuals must be dealt with swiftly. The team is called to a halt and the rebel is brought to heel with a few blows of the whip handle. If the agitator has inspired an all-out revolt then the blows rain down with vigour on them all. The dogs get the message and the handles pay the price.

Poor devils. The dogs have a grim existence over winter, though they are seemingly content to wander in the cold and dark during the day. A few have discovered that they can steal into the new underground toilet and feast on whatever's left by the men. It's a disgusting habit that nonetheless keeps the area clean and free of smells. A few have gone further afield in search of delights. With no wildlife to harass at this time of year, a few of the more intrepid dogs head inland to investigate the unfulfilling emptiness of the barrier. Most return after a day or two. Thankfully Madeiro finally has. Some do not.

Most absences are picked up at feeding time. Nobody gets fed until all the dogs are safely tied up for the night in their allotted tent. There's howling and fighting aplenty, but finally each man has his fifteen or so dogs under control and dishes out the chunks of meat and blubber or dried fish, depending on the day. Few of them like the fish and they are harder to wrangle into line on alternate nights. The more intelligent among them have worked out the drill and have come to recognise what's being served by its means of delivery.

Forever the prankster, Helmer has turned the tables on his team, and taken to serving fish from the meat box. The double-crossed dogs take their frustration out on the meat tent the next day. Surrounded by a six-foot-high snow wall and encircled by buried lengths of barbed wire, it's quite safe. There's little a dog can do other than lift its leg in protest.

CHAPTER THIRTY

Amundsen wakes with a start. The noise. There it is again. A distant vibration. His feet tingle with unease. He strains to hear it. Yes, the unmistakable rumble of motors, the sound travelling on the wind in and out of earshot. Captain Scott's on the move. It's the only explanation. But at night? Here? Amundsen flings his feet over the side of his bunk. He must collect his thoughts. The noise erupts anew. This time from the bunk opposite. Despite the relief he feels at discovering the true source of the rumble, Amundsen flings a book in Helmer's direction. The snoring ceases.

Sleep does not return. How can it when such thoughts rouse worry in his mind? The motor sledges, the motor sledges, the motor sledges – round and round his anxiety spirals. Scott will win for sure with such technology on his side. *Skis and dogs – how can we ever compete?*

'My improved plan is this,' Amundsen announces at breakfast. 'We shall leave here by the middle of September.'

There are pancakes on the plates but no one's eating them.

'But that's a whole six weeks ahead of schedule,' says Johansen darkly.

'Well, it will be lighter at least,' says Helmer in a conciliatory tone.

'It's before the sun returns though.' Johansen shakes his head at such absurdity. 'Nansen and I set off too early. In the Arctic. We were pounded by the cold. We had to turn back. It was impossible to carry on.'

Amundsen ignores Johansen's concerns. 'Eight men, seven sledges, eighty-four dogs. We'll stop at our depot at 80 degrees for a couple of days, feed the dogs up – as much meat as they can handle – then carry on to 81 degrees where we'll rest the dogs, feed them up again. We'll build ourselves some igloos and dry out our gear while we wait for the sun.'

They wonder if winter has got the better of the chief. He seems a trifle unhinged. Nobody dares say a word.

Amundsen continues. 'I also think it advisable that we undertake a practice journey, to give our gear a thorough going over.'

'Haven't we already done that, with the depot-laying?' asks Prestrud, a little uneasily.

'We'll head east into King Edward VII Land, somewhere we haven't been yet. New terrain, new challenges. It'll be good training.'

Sverre coughs. 'The dogs won't like it. It's still too cold for them, I think.'

'We've only finished three sledges.' Bjaaland looks at Stubberud for support but the carpenter merely stares into his coffee.

Oscar feels a shiver run down his spine. It's been well below minus 40 degrees Celsius. Surely the temperature will need to be much higher before heading south.

'How about we put it to the vote?' Amundsen's gaze challenges the table. *This is a good test of loyalty*, he thinks.

'I'm abstaining,' says Lindstrøm, leaning back in his chair with his palms raised. 'Not my department.'

'Come on, lads!' Amundsen slaps the table. He's angry now. 'Give me a show of hands.'

No hands.

Johansen speaks. 'I think it's nuts.' He didn't need to say it. And judging by Amundsen's steely expression, he shouldn't have. But it's out now, on the table – a flicker of dissent.

Chapter Thirty-One

For the second time in a month the leader asks his men to vote on a trial run. Nobody will agree to his unnecessary training journey to the east. That is not to say the men have lost faith in the rational mind of their leader. Mostly they put it down to jitters. It's clear that Amundsen is done with waiting. Unpleasant as the atmosphere around the table turns once they fail to approve Amundsen's proposal for a second time, they all acknowledge his reasoning is sound. This is a race after all. The overhaul of their equipment is largely finished, their sledges are packed. Clothing, skis, tents are in pristine condition and the dogs are fat and frustrated with pent-up energy. But it's still only August and the skies are still dark. Amundsen's impatience is not contagious. For the men, suicide is not so appealing.

Prestrud's occupying the table as usual. Oscar happily shares the light. There are only a couple of books he hasn't read from the library that Lindstrøm keeps in the loft above the kitchen. He's consumed more than seventy over the last few months. He may need to start from the beginning and re-read the various volumes if he is to keep himself amused. He already knows he won't be taking away any holiday reading to the pole. Each man has a paltry 10-kilo allowance and that's accounted for with extra socks, snow goggles, spare underwear and mittens, reindeer kamiks, a face mask for blizzards and a pocket mirror to check for signs of frostbite.

Prestrud looks up from his workings and shakes his head. 'August twenty-fourth.'

Oscar looks up. 'What did you say?'

'Our new start date – August twenty-fourth. It's so soon.'

'You're the one who told him.' Oscar gives a sneer. 'Said that's the day the sun reappears over the horizon.'

'Well, I could hardly keep it from him.' Prestrud sits up defensively. 'The information's all here written down – see!' Thrusting the Nautical Almanac across the table, Prestrud inadvertently knocks over the oil lamp.

Oscar leaps from his seat as the oil spreads towards him then ignites. Neither man knows quite what to do. The almanac is ablaze and there's nothing nearby to smother the flames. The commotion brings Lindstrøm from the kitchen.

Prestrud flaps hopelessly at the almanac, seriously considering using his body to save the precious volume. Lindstrøm throws a damp towel which lands with a heroic flop right on target.

With barely concealed horror, Prestrud peels back the fabric to assess the damage. Lindstrøm tut-tuts his way over to the scene of destruction.

'Is it okay?' Oscar asks, feeling partially responsible for baiting the navigator.

Prestrud releases a deep breath. 'It's burnt right up to our day of departure – if you can believe that.'

Lindstrøm whistles and wanders back into the kitchen. *It's a sign alright*, he thinks to himself, *just not a particularly good one.*

CHAPTER THIRTY-TWO

'I can't understand why the English have such disdain for skis and dogs. And they pour scorn on fur clothing. We'll show them. We'll demonstrate the full extent of the knowledge and understanding that has propelled the Norwegians to the forefront of polar exploration!'

Amundsen is not a boastful man. This is more a war cry, a limbering up before the dash south. 'It's so interesting, in his account of reaching furthest south, Shackleton pronounces that fur is unnecessary and that a wool and a windproof layer are sufficient. But then he complains of the cold!'

'Well, aren't we lucky then?' adds Helmer, his sarcasm clear. 'If it weren't for Shackleton's stupidity, he'd have made it to the pole and I'd be back in Norway cuddling my wife.'

'And where would you rather be?' Sverre asks.

There's a pause as Helmer pretends to consider the question deeply. 'Here, of course!'

The men roar with laughter.

Amundsen quietens the room. 'I'm not saying Shackleton and his companions lacked courage and strength. I just can't share his view that the Great Ice Barrier is such a mysterious place. It's obviously a glacier. Massive to be sure, but a glacier nonetheless.'

August has been a frenzy of last-minute activity. The major adjustments to equipment and packing are now finished and attention has turned to myriad smaller tasks – making scales for weighing provisions, producing lighter tent poles, redesigning ski bindings. Oscar has fashioned large windproof layers to fit over reindeer trousers and Helmer has made leather snow goggles. Sverre has re-soldered all the lids of the tins of paraffin to prevent any evaporation – the evil vapours in his fuel storage are proof that significant leakage has already taken place. Once again each man has stripped back his individual snow boots, intent on perfecting the fit while he still has the luxury of a table, chair and warmth enough to wield a needle and thread. In an unpopular move, Amundsen has decreed that each man will sew a sledging harness for himself.

'You can't be serious,' Bjaaland scoffs with incredulity.

But Amundsen is serious. Should the unthinkable happen and all the dogs perish, the men will provide pulling power.

The day before departure passes quickly. Using a makeshift crane, the men winch seven fully laden sledges out from the underground workshop and into the light of day. The dogs are harnessed to the heavy loads and sent up onto the barrier with the chief leading the way on skis. The trip takes two hours. On arrival at the designated 'starting point', the dogs are released and sent home, and yet a few choose to remain by the sledges, showing a degree of loyalty that puts the men to shame, knowing as they do that few dogs will survive. Spirits are high that night. There's a certain luxury in having started the polar journey and returning home to Fatty for dinner.

According to Prestrud's astronomical tables the sun is due to reappear the next day, but it is still fearfully cold. Sverre recounts how his breath turned to ice in mid-air and rustled as it fell to the ground. Everyone saw how Amundsen's nostrils froze that morning. The solid ice cubes completely restricted his flow of air. The coughing and clearing and shaking of his head would have been comical if not for the chief's foul mood. He is beyond frustrated. To depart in such conditions is unwise. Their grand departure will be postponed for another five days.

'Praise the Lord for small mercies,' breathes Bjaaland.

'I'm going to make a sandwich for the sun,' says Lindstrøm.

'A sandwich?' snorts Stubberud. 'What does the sun need with a sandwich?'

'Leave him be. I've learnt never to question Fatty and his mysterious ways.' Amundsen folds his arms across his chest.

The following day the dogs end up eating Lindstrøm's offering. The sun has returned after its long winter absence, but fails to cast any of its rays from behind an ominous fortress of cloud on the horizon.

The days drag by. Each day colder than the last. Minus 52, minus 53 degrees. The men are restless, increasingly worried about their chances of withstanding the penetrating cold of early spring. Resentment surfaces. *Must we really do this? Is he serious about setting off?* Voices never rise above whispers, but Amundsen's not fooled; their unease is palpable. Emotion has no place in his decision-making. Logic must prevail. When the chief again revises their date of departure, it is the prevailing winter temperatures he cites rather than any dire misgivings the men themselves have raised.

Seven o'clock on the morning of 4 September is their scheduled departure, but once the day arrives, so does a savage howling wind that sends so much drift into the air that the men cannot see their hands in front of their faces. Amundsen expresses his rage in a silence so profound that not even Lindstrøm attempts carefree banter. Three days pass. The atmosphere in the hut is tomblike.

'For goodness' sake, let's just go!' shouts Helmer, thumping the table in exasperation.

And the next day they do, whether they want to or not.

Chapter Thirty-Three

Amundsen issues a cloud of expletives. Almost immediately ice crystals gather on his hood, the long tips of fur becoming more like spiked winter foliage with every breath. There is nothing remotely pleasant about their journey. For the first time in years, Amundsen is cold. Not even his pride can keep him warm. The cold feels like a personal insult, a hateful jeering slight against his character, against his leadership. In this realm of deficits, where a slow subtraction of feeling is the norm, reindeer clothing can no longer offer protection. Even the milky speck in the sky that was once the sun cannot hold its own and shrinks into the gloom. Steeling himself, Amundsen drives onward.

Again he swears and shouts, 'Go home!'

The puppies are oblivious to the abuse hurled in their direction. Playful and eager, these three pups from Camilla's second litter do not understand the serious intent of this outing. Entertainment is their sole motivation. Nothing breaks their stride, not the cold, nor the wind, nor the fact that food is not forthcoming. Mile after mile they continue their lighthearted gambolling beside their mother's sledge. Helmer serves up a sharp lick of his whip but still the puppies refuse to go home. The other dogs are unsettled, resentful of the youngsters' larking while they chafe in their traces. One team sees a chance to lunge at the annoying threesome but instead of teaching them a lesson, the attackers end up embroiled in warfare with another team. Sverre's teeth chatter as he attempts to untangle the traces, with Helmer and Johansen yanking on the dogs. It's an hour of fumbling with frozen hands. Despite stamping their feet and slapping their sides with increasing violence, the other men get desperately cold standing for so long in one place.

The chief is a man obsessed by one goal to the exclusion of all others. Nothing must stand in his way. Amundsen loads his gun and shoots all three pups.

Through days of horror the men stay the course, even as their clothing becomes rigid with ice and the sledges grow a fur-like layer of rime frost from waves of dogs' breath. The cold saps strength and adventurousness and any sense of shared purpose. Each man is an island of suffering that not even a night's rest can relieve. Sleep has become an unattainable luxury. It's as if the body, unable to trust itself to wake up, will not allow the kind of deep slumber the men so need. Even the gin Amundsen has packed for their moment of celebration at the pole has given up the ghost.

'The flask's cracked,' he says, incredulous.

'The aquavit's still okay. Well, frozen solid, but the bottle's still intact,' says Helmer.

The men thaw the bottle slowly, turning it round and round in the precious warmth radiating from the Primus. Under normal circumstances no one would be permitted to take a drink, but it's minus 56 degrees and the men are desperate for even the superficial heat of strong spirits. Johansen, who has so far made a point of abstaining, sucks the alcohol greedily into his frigid system without much effect. Outside, the dogs whimper.

'I am colder than I have ever been in my entire life,' says Bjaaland through gritted teeth. He remains completely still in his sleeping bag for fear of letting in more chill.

Finally it is so cold that the liquid in the compasses freezes.

'Let's call it quits.' Amundsen's jaw clenches as if in distaste. 'There's no point risking men and dogs.'

Relief crackles among the party. It's been four days. They still must get to the 80 degrees depot to dump their supplies, but the thought of home provides them with the keenest motivation and they cover the distance in a day and a half.

A number of dogs grow too weak to continue. Rasmus falls dead in his tracks, signalling the end of the Three Musketeers. Another collapses mid-stride. When not on the move they repeatedly lift their paws off the snow in a display of frozen anguish. There is no need of the whip; the remaining dogs instinctively flee from the perilous south in the direction of home.

'My watch has stopped,' says Sverre.

'My foot's so swollen,' Stubberud says, fear ringing in his voice. 'I think I've got frostbite.'

A closer inspection reveals even more damage than he thought.

'My heel's come off,' says Helmer with detached fascination. He holds up the wad of waxy flesh, a grisly curio. It's a horrifying sight, particularly for Stubberud and Prestrud who wonder if that is what is in store for them.

Amundsen is horrified it has come to this. The next morning they rise at five and are away by seven. The weather is fast deteriorating. They must make Framheim in one stretch. The group splits in two. Helmer, Oscar and Amundsen lead off, setting a cracking pace with their largely empty sledges bouncing across the snow. Soon the only sign of them is their tracks, which Stubberud follows diligently. But the carpenter's pace soon slows until his dogs simply refuse to advance. The aching cold stiffens his limbs; his frostbitten foot feels dead in his boot. He sits on his sledge and considers his predicament – no food, no tent, no fuel – while the weather thickens around him like a boiling cauldron of white. For some time he waits, hoping for Sverre, Bjaaland or anyone else behind him to help. But when a man finally arrives, he shoots past in a blur.

'Alright?' Bjaaland yells backwards, rattling past at speed.

'What the heck!' he yells back. To not even consider stopping to help – Stubberud's mightily offended. But the sight and scent of Bjaaland's dog team whizzing by has enlivened his own dogs and suddenly they're on their feet and keen to mount a pursuit. It's a minor miracle and they do not stop until they reach home.

Sverre covers distance as best he can, well behind Bjaaland and Stubberud. Slow and steady, he blocks out all thoughts of the two men trailing behind him. *With this beastly cold strangling us, it's each man for himself,* he reasons. *Johansen is strong, more experienced than anyone. And Prestrud, well . . . frankly, he's the lucky one on skis without a dog team to worry about.*

In truth, Prestrud has fallen over 20 kilometres behind the others. Bent almost double against the wind, he is close to giving in.

Sverre hears the cries off in the distance but he doesn't want to believe his ears. He doesn't want to turn around, even though he knows it's Johansen. Mostly he doesn't want to stop, so he ignores the cries and carries on.

For the past six hours Johansen has driven his team like a maniac intent on squeezing every last drop of life from their bodies. His own body is nearing its limits. He's severely dehydrated, frozen to his core and exhausted beyond measure.

'Sverre!' he shouts.

Sverre slows his team even though he might not be able to get them going again. 'Don't make me wait,' he implores Johansen. 'I don't want to die out here.'

'And Prestrud?' comes the angry reply from the iced-up hood of Johansen's anorak. 'He's on his own. He won't make it if we don't wait for him.'

'*You* wait. Why do you need me?' Sverre can't believe how unreasonable Johansen is becoming.

'We don't have anything! No tent, no food. They've left us with nothing,' Johansen is shouting into the wind now.

Sverre fumbles a tent free from his sledge and thrusts it at Johansen. 'This is all I've got,' he states. He whips his dogs into renewed escape and the whiteness swallows them whole.

'Where could they be?' Oscar's question hangs in the air. They'd all like an answer, if only to assuage their own guilt. Having secured their own safe retreat to Framheim, covering 64 kilometres in nine hours, the men's thoughts now dwell on their two missing companions.

'They've got a tent, at least.' Sverre takes a sip of hot chocolate even though it will not sit well in his churning stomach.

All around them are untidy piles of iced-up clothing, hurriedly cast off and now in varying stages of thaw. The air is thick with the earthy smell of wet fur and the acrid stench of stress. Nobody makes an effort to clean it up. What's the point? There'll be more mess to tidy once the others arrive home, assuming they do – eventually.

'Cold enough to catch your death out there,' says Lindstrøm amid the hush that lingers over the table. For once there are no smiles. His comment has captured the mood and crystallised their worst fear: that Johansen and Prestrud are dead and it is entirely their fault.

'Time to turn in, I think,' says Amundsen crisply.

CHAPTER THIRTY-FOUR

Winter menaces the two stragglers. It is a heartless beast. Tooth and claw, it will fight to claim their last breaths; but Johansen is every bit its match. Drawing on the blackness inside himself, the empty bits where love and hope and glory once lived, he fights on. Bitterness and hate swell in his chest; they've struggled to find expression until now.

Leaving us to die out here. Johansen's resentment nestles deeper into his core.

Johansen knows one thing: he must get Prestrud to shelter. It's clear his feet are badly frostbitten. The man can hardly propel himself forward. His staggering, his mumbling avowals – it all points to hypothermia.

'I'm sorry, I'm so sorry,' he slurs in waves of contrition that are totally out of character.

'Keep moving,' Johansen urges.

They've had their moments, Prestrud and Johansen. The deep division that occurred during depot-laying has never had a chance to mend. None of it matters out here. Only Johansen's dark loathing for their leader matters. It drives him ever onward, head bowed against the squalls of driving snow.

After midnight the temperature stabilises at minus 51 degrees. They are getting close, but other perils lie in wait for the two men.

'Why are we stopping?' moans Prestrud.

'No tracks.'

Johansen knows they're fast approaching the barrier edge and that it's so dark they'll likely miss the narrow path to lead them down safely. A 50-foot drop cannot be negotiated, he knows that for sure. And yet where is the way down? The fog is at its thickest. The compass is useless. Framheim lies somewhere on the edge of this oblivion.

'Devil take you, Amundsen,' he fumes.

CHAPTER THIRTY-FIVE

The fire's lit, the kitchen door opens. The cook flings down the plates and cutlery on the table before rounding off his performance with his customary finale – the dropping of spoons from a height into each of the men's enamel mugs.

'Quit it, Fatty.'

'Of all mornings. We deserve a sleep-in.'

'Why you softies, I was up until one last night waiting for the boys. You don't hear me complaining.' Lindstrøm retreats to the kitchen to do battle with the coffee mill.

There's movement in the bunks. Some groaning. A little slower than normal, the men emerge and set about their various morning rituals – washing, dressing and heading outside for a minute or two to guess the temperature – it's just like any other morning except there is a heaviness in the air and hardly a word is spoken. Stubberud is limping badly. So is Helmer. There is no laughter or small talk or joking as they sit down.

Amundsen takes a sip of his coffee and regards Johansen over the rim of his mug. 'What took you so long?'

'WHAT TOOK US SO LONG?' Johansen shouts. 'You left us for dead!' Hatred gushes forth unabashed. 'Call yourself a leader? You're nothing but a coward. Save yourself! To hell with anyone else.'

The men shrink from the table. Such vehemence directed at the chief – it's unthinkable.

'No leader should ever abandon his team!' Fine specks of spittle fly in Amundsen's direction. Johansen pauses, mustering his thoughts, his mouth working, his eyes fixed on the mask of the chief's face. He starts anew, 'Prestrud was left. Neither of us had anything. It was madness. Blundering like idiots out there. We lost our bearings in fog. We'd lost the light. We're only alive because we heard the dogs barking outside the hut. We had to follow the bloody howling of dogs to get home. Clearly no one was coming to look for us. It's a disgrace.' There's a pause. 'You're a disgrace.'

A profound silence descends. Johansen is right. But the hut is so small and his voice is so loud. Embarrassment prevents anyone from speaking up. Prestrud simply looks at his plate and wishes for it all to be over.

'It was madness to set out so early in the season. You're going to kill us all with your plans. You don't have a clue what you're doing.' Johansen's words trail off. He shakes his head.

Amundsen takes it all, his eyes resting on Johansen's weather-beaten complexion with studied indifference. To be thus challenged, and with an audience. Does Johansen really think he'll get away with this? Mutinous. It's a defining moment. His authority must not be called into question.

'How dare you?' Amundsen's voice is even but forceful. 'I'll have no more of your slanderous talk. It is nobody's fault other than your own. You failed to keep pace with the rest of the group. It is your failing, sir. It was *not* my priority to ensure you had a tent on your sledge. I had men who required medical attention. As far as I was concerned that took precedence over checking on the likes of you, Hjalmar Johansen. *That* was my priority.'

Johansen scoffs. 'You and your so-called priorities be damned.'

Johansen has let humiliation and bitterness and a whole raft of other ugly feelings he cannot define get the better of him. Yes, he was opposed to setting out so early, yes he had the weakest dog team, yes he had no provisions, but to say things that cannot be unsaid – that is far from prudent. This was his time – to make his name shine once more, to bask in the fame that was once his, to rehabilitate himself, to move beyond the unhappiness of losing his wife, his kids, and his self-control. This was his time to prove his worth, to the world and to himself.

Amundsen's words are unhurried. 'Hjalmar Johansen, you have overstepped the mark. Given you hold my leadership in such low regard and have been so forthright in your criticisms of this expedition, you leave me no option but to remove you from our journey to the South Pole.'

CHAPTER THIRTY-SIX

5 OCTOBER 1911 – BUENOS AIRES

'Back to the bergs,' says Captain Nilsen, passing his callused hands down the front of his shirt and surveying the muddy waters of the Rio de la Plata for the last time. Spring is already upon them and summer will surely follow on its heels, but where they're heading, he'll need his woollens, waterproofs and reindeer-skin anorak.

Much has been left to Nilsen's discretion once they set sail from the Bay of Whales in mid-February. Amundsen's only request is that the ship be back as early as possible in 1912.

It was never meant to be a pleasure cruise. With barely enough men to sail the ship, the crew have battled waves that reach the sky, hurricane winds, snow squalls and fog while navigating around more than 500 icebergs on their journey across the Southern Pacific to Cape Horn and up the coast of South America to Buenos Aires. A full set of her sails completely worn out, the *Fram* had shuddered into port, with the direst challenge still ahead.

'We arrived as paupers and leave as princes,' says Lieutenant Gjertsen cheerily.

'I feel more like Noah,' says Nilsen, looking rather forlornly about him at the sheep and pigs. Housed in a weatherproof hut on deck, the animals communicate their confusion about their new surroundings in a far more muted fashion than the dogs on the voyage from Norway, and leave a lot less mess to clean up.

Nilsen does not need the crew to remind him of the agony of their arrival in Buenos Aires two months after leaving the ice. It wasn't so much that they were paupers – they were more like beggars, with barely enough provisions to feed themselves and certainly no money to purchase even a side of beef. To make matters worse, the expedition funds that should have been waiting for them had not arrived.

'I do hope Amundsen has found a mighty mountain in Antarctica that he can name in honour of our beloved compatriot and benefactor.'

Gjertsen agrees. 'God bless Don Pedro.'

Don Pedro Christophersen, Norwegian businessman and diplomat, had certainly answered the call in their hour of need, not only supplying provisions and fuel but also generously covering the costs of repainting the ship, refurbishing her engine and repairing the damage that is inevitable when a ship travels such immense distances around the globe without dropping anchor.

Don Pedro has also offered to send a rescue mission should the *Fram* not reappear with her full contingent by a certain date. *Well, we won't let it come to that*, thinks Nilsen, thrusting out his jaw.

Their course is set. They'll travel back along their original westward route, doing battle with the Roaring Forties and Furious Fifties yet again, rounding the Horn and passing within sight of the Kerguelen Islands, where they will yet attempt to land.

Nilsen is impatient. He's fulfilled his end of the bargain and even completed the oceanographical cruise in the South Atlantic that Amundsen asked for. A total of 891 water samples and temperature readings have been collected at various locations, as well as countless phials of sand and silt from the seabed and over 190 specimens of plankton. They've already been packaged up and sent to Norway. *Whoever wants them is welcome to them* thinks Nilsen. *I've done my part.*

The captain hopes that Amundsen has done his part.

'He'll be thinking of setting out, I should think,' Nilsen says to Gjertsen. 'Amundsen needs to prove himself for all our sakes. I don't much like the idea of returning home empty-handed. Not with Amundsen's little change of plan to explain to the nation.'

'Touch wood, it all works out,' Gjertsen says.

Nilsen grasps the wheel with enthusiasm. He has no desire to take sole responsibility for the expedition. But that is what will happen if Amundsen has perished during his quest for glory. Nilsen gives an involuntary shudder. Of course, a worse scenario would be if Framheim (and all who have made it home these past nine months) has crumbled into the sea. The captain quickly steers his thoughts away from possible catastrophes.

'I wonder how my little friend Madeiro is getting on,' he says suddenly.

CHAPTER THIRTY-SEVEN

After September's false start and the uncomfortable atmosphere that has persisted in the hut since Johansen's outburst, it's a relief to be in the fresh air and on the move again. Helmer, Oscar, Bjaaland and Sverre are the chosen ones; Prestrud, Stubberud and Johansen will stay behind with Lindstrøm.

Despite being the only man (aside from the chief) to escape the debilitating effects of frostbite on the abortive September journey, Johansen is firmly on the outer. Offering his best wishes to the departing men and shaking Amundsen's hand in farewell, he suppresses all feelings of resentment. The irony of being 100 per cent healthy and yet left behind with the invalids is not lost on him. What would Nansen say?

To add insult to injury, Johansen is now under the command of Lieutenant Prestrud. It's a move designed to punish and humiliate him. Everyone knows his knowledge and experience are far superior. Together they will undertake a pre-Christmas excursion to the as-yet-unexplored King Edward VII Land, while the others take on the South Pole. Stubberud's been assigned as their third man. He is bitter but can do little to change his fate. His frostbitten heel still gives him trouble. To be excluded is a blow to his pride and his ambitions – he has put his entire heart and soul into readying the team for victory, and his life has been on hold for more than a year.

A strong southerly headwind and thick driving snow characterise the polar party's first days. With no features to fix on, no hints as to their position, each man drifts in and out of his thoughts. The hours dissolve into white nothingness, mile after mile after mile. They've made this journey three times already and yet there is nothing familiar about their route. Old tracks show up from time to time but never with enough conviction to offer definitive guidance. Helmer commands the leading sledge with one eye on his compass and the other on the sledge-meter. Twice they've strayed off course. Once into the treacherous eastern crevasse field encountered during the third depot-laying journey. A superstitious man would say it is Johansen's revenge.

Sheltering at their 82 degrees depot, the five men are at the boundary of their knowledge. Beyond the tent is an unknown land full of peril. The extreme physical challenges they will face in the months ahead will test the limits of their endurance and mental grit. Everyone is aware that death could claim one or all of their number, but nobody is going to deny the excitement they each feel; there's a race to win.

With their sledges stocked up with enough provisions to last ninety-nine days, the long road ahead seems not so daunting. The 'road', such as it is, has been plotted on the map and is represented by a heavy line, straight as an arrow, pointing south. Should any obstacles lie in the way – mountains, valleys or impassable glaciers – they'll only find out en route. It's the men's unspoken hope that their chosen line will rise in a gradual fashion all the way to the polar plateau without offering much resistance. Amundsen knows that even though Scott will be sticking to the route taken by Shackleton up the Beardmore Glacier, he will face his own fair share of risks. It's likely that the Norwegians will have to navigate similar terrain to pierce the Transantarctic Mountains. They've got alpine ropes, but any obstacles requiring serious mountaineering skills will put an end to their dreams.

'We've been lucky,' says Oscar.

There's a general murmur of agreement. With each passing day they appreciate in starker relief the monumental scale of their ambitions and the potential for it all to end in tragedy.

'We've been lucky? Don't you mean me?' Helmer scoffs, recalling how heavily he had fallen across the wide gash of a crevasse. His skis had got tangled in the pulley hook of the dogs' traces. Locked at a right angle by his skis and unable to haul himself to safety, Helmer was rendered powerless. Of course his team used the delay to launch into a vicious brawl. Half-in, half-out, the heavy sledge had teetered dangerously closer to the edge with each jarring movement of the dogs. It took four men more than half an hour in gusting winds to bring the situation under control, sweating, swearing, fearing the loss of the sledge, their provisions, a team of the best dogs and a man into the bargain.

'What about me?' protests Bjaaland, who almost lost his entire sledge down a yawning chasm in the midst of Johansen's crevasse field. The rescue had pushed the entire team to the brink of exhaustion. Finally the sledge had been unloaded in its precarious position, crate by crate, at great personal risk to Oscar who had volunteered to be lowered into the hole.

'Looking down and seeing those horrible spikes of ice. If Bjaaland hadn't broken every bone in his body on the way down, he'd have been impaled.' Oscar whistles in unpleasant recollection. 'Where the dogs had crossed was the narrowest part of the crevasse. Either side of that, it opened up wider than a street. None of us would have escaped if we'd been spread out.' He stirs his bowl of pemmican, blowing the steam away with his own misty breath.

'Down there you're out of the blasted wind at least.' Sverre's laugh develops into a dry cough.

'Do you think the dogs can tell where to cross?' Oscar asks.

Sverre frowns. 'Not sure about that.'

'Dumb luck,' adds Amundsen.

Considering the dangers, the dogs are performing well. Two have been shot. One for being too scrawny, the other for being too fat. Neither could keep up the pace of the other dogs, who dash off each morning with such a lust for life that the men have allowed themselves to be towed behind the sledges on their skis – a luxury that will no doubt be short-lived.

A daily average of 27 kilometres is a most respectable distance, particularly when achieved in one stretch without stopping for food or drink. Some days the surface is heavy, impeding the dogs' forward momentum. Other days the surface is sticky like glue. Still other days the snow is grainy and loose. On the rare days when it is firm underfoot, it is almost a pleasure to be out. There is similar variation in the weather. It can be minus 35 degrees one day, minus 10 the next. Not surprisingly, the men are attuned to even the mildest changes in temperature, especially when nature calls.

Amundsen decides they will build a cairn every 5 kilometres. It will make navigating home a little less random and save on time, as they won't need to take observations and calculate their position. They'll also establish a depot for every degree of latitude they gain, leaving a portion of their provisions at each stop, which will cut down on the weight of the sledges and the burden on the dogs. They will soon start to lose condition. This next stage will be far from pleasant for these unfortunate creatures, soon to be reduced to cannibals. Competing in a race of their own, the dogs will need to earn the right to life. According to Amundsen's calculations, of the forty-two dogs that set out, only twelve will return.

CHAPTER THIRTY-EIGHT

Amundsen points one ski pole south. There can be no mistake where he means to direct the men's gaze. The landscape could not be more different from the monotonous barrier surface they've spent the best part of a month crossing. The Transantarctic Mountains are like the fortifications holding back the vast polar ice cap; a daunting prospect for the most accomplished mountaineer. Somehow the Norwegians will have to find a way through the maze of summits with their dogs and sledges.

'Never thought I'd be excited to see bare rock,' says Helmer.

'Reminds me of the glaciers back home,' Amundsen says admiringly.

Helmer just squints in the bright sunshine.

Amundsen's eyes don't stray from the view. 'Did I ever tell you about the little adventure I had with my brother on Hardangervidda? I nearly died.'

Helmer doesn't ask for details. He's silent. The gigantic peaks stretching out east to west before him present quite a foe.

'That's our way up,' says Amundsen simply.

Rather than an orderly route south, the glacier presents a jumbled mess of obstacles and pitfalls. Thankfully the weather is still and clear, but having to guide the dog teams so carefully around jagged blocks of ice, gaping holes and frightful chasms will slow their progress significantly. Planning will only take them so far at this critical stage of the journey. To navigate successfully through this mountain range they'll need a fair dollop of luck. Amundsen hates the very thought. Expect the unexpected, plan for the worst – this is his personal credo; however, it cannot guarantee their success in this instance.

'Sixty days' provisions, that's all we take.' Amundsen directs the unloading. All unnecessary weight is stripped and cached.

'I hope we make it back within your timeframe,' sighs Bjaaland. 'Else we'll all be going on a diet.'

Nervous laughter ripples through the company.

'Keep your jokes to yourself,' snaps Amundsen. 'They're not funny.'

Bjaaland straightens his back and catches Oscar's eye. The look passing between the men says it all.

Uncertainty is a heavy burden for Amundsen. More so than for any other man merely seeking personal glory. He faces an immense cost of failure. Thoughts of Scott and his motor sledges continue to torment him like an out-of-reach itch. The British could well be chugging their way to victory by now, having followed Shackleton's well-documented route up the Beardmore Glacier.

And here we are, striking out into unknown territory, Amundsen stews. Sharing moments of self-doubt is not in his nature. Neither is losing. For now, he will keep his anxiety concealed behind a curtain of ill-humour and irritability.

After so long skiing on the flat, the men tackle the uphill slopes in a clumsy fashion. The first few days of climbing through loose deep powder are arduous and they struggle to develop technique. At least there is the thrill of being the first people to see this dramatic landscape, and the novelty of naming vast swathes of this newly discovered land after kings, dignitaries, benefactors and members of the expedition. As they venture higher up and deeper into the mountains, Captain Nilsen, Fridtjof Nansen and

Queen Maud are the obvious winners – even Amundsen's housekeeper Betty has had a peak named in her honour. At night in the tent Amundsen announces that their route will henceforth be named the Axel Heiberg Glacier, after a wealthy sponsor. There are grunts of acknowledgement but ultimately dinner holds more interest. They are all exhausted.

Bjaaland is one man at home in the mountains. The uphill skiing that the others are still trying to perfect is an effortless ballet for the champion skier. Amundsen has sent him ahead of the dogs, part encouraging presence, part human prey for the eager teams to chase down. Often the slope is so steep that the men harness up twenty dogs to get one sledge moving. Each dog claws its way up the slope, panting, its belly low to the snow. Try as they might, they've yet to catch Bjaaland, but their ardour has carried them over a lot of difficult ground in an impressively short time.

As well as steep climbs, there have been numerous descents – some of them hundreds of metres in length. Every descent elicits a chorus of groans. A spot of downhill would normally pass for entertainment, but in the current context it is nothing but a cursed necessity. When you've fought so hard for uphill victory, it hurts to give up even a metre of altitude. Helmer wraps rope around the sledge runners to ensure they don't pick up too much speed on the way down. Trying to control a rampaging dog team and a sledge weighing several hundred kilograms involves nerves of steel and certainly the presence of mind to get out of the way should another team come barrelling out of control. Capsizing would signal disaster. Stubberud's lovingly honed sledging boxes do not have the structural integrity to survive an impact.

Every morning the men step from the tent, alive with a sense of wonderment at the majesty of their surroundings, but the feelings of awe fade as muscles that were pushed to their limits the day before start to complain in earnest. They still don't know where they're going or if their chosen route will deliver them to the polar plateau. Every day the distance seems greater, the challenge all the more unreasonable. The sun beats down without respite, its white acid light reflecting off every imaginable surface. Their lips are dry and cracked and thirst is a constant. Speaking only intensifies their dehydration, so they abandon conversation unless absolutely necessary.

'Should've kept to the east,' Bjaaland says.

Amundsen doesn't slacken his pace, instead points the way forward with his pole.

'But it's pointless. We'll need to backtrack.'

Refusing to stop, Amundsen simply says, 'The compass points south.'

'There's no sense to it,' Bjaaland complains. He's thoroughly sick of getting to the end of a strenuous climb only to discover, when looking back over the terrain, that there was an easier way up.

For Amundsen it is like listening to the constant grizzling of a child, one who he prefers to ignore.

But Bjaaland craves a response. 'Your problem is you can't admit you're wrong,' he says dejectedly.

Now Amundsen stops. He regards Bjaaland in stern silence. When he finally speaks, his voice is chalky dry. 'Olav Bjaaland: on reaching the Antarctic plateau you will be relieved of your duties and return to Framheim.'

'What?' Bjaaland splutters. 'What have I done wrong?'

'Your negative attitude. You will return to Framheim.'

'But I don't know how.'

'Then Sverre will take you.'

It's like it was with Johansen, only, in the middle of nowhere, it's far worse. His first instinct is to object loudly, but Bjaaland can tell by the way Amundsen clenches his jaw that to argue now would have little effect. Bjaaland looks to Sverre, who is too far behind to have heard the exchange, but he'll soon know all about it.

'This is disgusting,' Sverre fumes to Bjaaland in the privacy of their tent later that evening. 'Two able-bodied men . . . and he wants to send us back? The man's got a screw loose.'

Bjaaland nods vigorously. 'We could die out there on our own.'

Even as Sverre and Bjaaland rail against their leader, Helmer and Oscar refuse to hear one bad word about the chief. Both men would follow him into the abyss if he asked for volunteers. Their confidence is not misplaced. Amundsen's sound planning and infinite patience in working out every last detail have brought them safely to 85.36 degrees south; the same principles will carry them forward to 90 degrees. It may feel an eternity since they set off from the barrier but it has only taken the team four days to travel 77 kilometres up the wholly uncharted Axel Heiberg Glacier.

'I've seen it all before,' says Helmer. 'The chief's just focused on his outcome. Bjaaland should ask for forgiveness and see what he says.'

Mentally and physically exhausted, Bjaaland has lost the naïve sense of adventure he felt on leaving Framheim. Good-natured conversation and camaraderie have been sacrificed to fatigue and anxiety. This is polar exploration, raw and unpleasant, and he's not sure it's for him. Even so, he'll not be deprived of victory at the pole after getting this far.

'I'm sorry,' says Bjaaland.

Amundsen does not look up from his diary.

'I really am so sorry. It won't happen again. I promise. I don't want to go back. I want to carry on to the pole.'

'Hindsight is a wonderful thing,' Amundsen sighs

as he notes down the various 'shortcuts' they've failed to spot from below. In time they'll be crossing back over here from the opposite direction and every bit of ground they can make up the better – however tired they feel now after climbing the Axel Heiberg Glacier, they will feel ten times more exhausted on their return from the pole. The men have earned two days of rest. There is a fearful challenge ahead of them.

'Very well, Bjaaland,' says Amundsen. 'You may stay.'

CHAPTER THIRTY-NINE

Amundsen recognises it as a failing, a weakness in his character, but he cannot take part in the slaughter. They've already christened this camp 'the Butcher's Shop'. It is too awful. His dogs. They have demonstrated unstinting loyalty, applying their vigour day after day for weeks on end to accomplish the selfish whim of man. Surrendering every ounce of energy hauling the provisions up the glacier, they have nothing left to offer up but their own flesh. If he and his men are to reach the South Pole, much will be due to the dogs.

Inside the tent Amundsen pumps the Primus to ease

the flow of fuel. Even though he's expecting it, the first gunshot makes him flinch. The abrupt violence of the sound seems out of place in the gloom of early evening, in such pristine surroundings. Echoing off the mountains, other shots ring out in quick succession. There is no need to count. Amundsen knows there will be twenty-four such reverberations, all eventually absorbed by the whistling of the wind and the howling of the survivors.

Feasting on the entrails of their former companions, most of the remaining dogs do not care where their latest meal comes from. For them, loyalty to fallen comrades cannot compete with desperate hunger. A few are reluctant at first, sniffing the bloody mounds suspiciously, then licking them, before eventually tucking in with gusto. The effort of the last few days has taken a lot out of them. Requiring more sustenance than their daily rations of pemmican deliver, the dogs will eat anything left lying on the snow and will happily stoop to thievery if an opportunity presents itself. Several days ago Amundsen had to wrestle one such villain to the ground and make him return the morsel he so brutally tore from another dog's mouth. It was a brave, if somewhat foolhardy, action on Amundsen's part. Viciousness has become a common trait. Among the eighteen strongest dogs who have been spared, another six will eventually be sacrificed to the cause – which ones is yet to be determined, but this is now very much a dog-eat-dog world.

When it comes to raging hunger, the men are little better off than the animals, and fall on their rations at the end of the day with single-minded focus and little in the way of conversation. Tonight should be no different. Having gone through the motions of lighting the stove and warming the tent, Amundsen surrenders all dinner preparations to Oscar.

'It's blowing out there now,' says Sverre. The last one to enter the tent for the evening, he removes his boots and peels back the multiple layers of stinking woollen socks. Nobody complains. Over the weeks, the men have grown more tolerant of the rich spectrum of odours emanating from their companions.

Amundsen looks up from his diary. 'Prevailing winds are from the south. The northerly slopes are all iced up. The ones facing south are completely free of snow.'

Helmer sighs, knowing they're going to get the same treatment. 'A southerly wind full in the face.'

'Well, we can pick up the pace now. Lighter sledges, better surface.' Amundsen offers what he hopes is an accurate assessment. He can't afford for the men to lose heart in the face of the most challenging section of their journey.

'I don't like our chances of setting off on schedule if these gales continue.' Sverre peers over Oscar's shoulder at the contents of the bubbling pot of pemmican.

'Well, let's hope it settles in the next forty-eight hours,' says Amundsen. 'The dogs need a chance to digest the good feed they've just had.'

'A good feed,' says Sverre. 'Just what I'm looking forward to.'

Oscar nods absent-mindedly as he considers the plate of what he assumes are the choicest cuts. As the evening's chef he has the special job of figuring out how to cook dog. He's never eaten it, let alone had to take responsibility for turning it into something palatable. Should he try to disguise its flavour? Cut it in small cubes so it's easy to swallow without too much thought as to what the poor creature's name was? Camilla? Madeiro? Oscar knows they'll not be eating those particular dogs tonight – but their turn could easily come somewhere down the line.

'I'd like to see Scott eating his motor sledges!' scoffs Helmer.

'What does dog taste like?' Oscar asks.

'Like meat.'

'Does it have a flavour, I mean?'

Helmer shrugs. 'Meat flavour.'

It may have been a source of anguish to kill the dogs, but now that the evil deed is done, nobody seems fussed about eating them. For Helmer, Sverre and Amundsen, tonight's stew is just another of many dog-meat dinners consumed over their years conducting business in polar regions. It will be a first for Bjaaland, but the skier appears not the least bit squeamish about the prospect. He's just as fixated on filling his empty belly as the dogs themselves.

Oscar doesn't enjoy handling the meat. He's already had a hand in the killing and the ghastly job of skinning the poor brutes. Now he wants rid of it. Chopping the flesh roughly, Oscar drops it from thumb and forefinger into the pot of bubbling pemmican.

'Soup,' he says, trying to convince himself that the dish has nothing to do with the animals that carried them up the steep glacier.

'You don't need to cook it forever,' Helmer says gruffly. 'Dish up, I'm starving.'

Oscar gives the pot another stir. 'It's barely cooked. It'll be tough as old shoe leather.'

'Chewy's fine.' Amundsen extends his cup in the direction of food.

'I'm ready,' adds Bjaaland, freeing up his utensils from the bag.

Oscar can see that the urging will not cease until each man cradles his serving of dog stew under his nose. Carefully he ladles out steaming spoonfuls.

'Where's all the meat?' Helmer complains. 'You've only given me pemmican with all the dried veggie bits.'

'Hold your horses. It's down the bottom.' Oscar fails

to hide his exasperation. 'Drink your soup, then you can let loose on the meat.'

The sounds of slurping are followed by immediate feedback of the sort any chef would welcome.

'This is delicious.'

'Mmmm, outstanding.'

'Such rich flavour.'

'Just like my wife's, only better!'

'Your wife cooks dog?' Bjaaland asks Helmer incredulously.

It's nice to share a laugh after many weeks of stress and sniping. Amid the uncharacteristic jocularity, Oscar takes his first tentative sip. The flavour is indeed rich with a gamey intensity that is otherwise lacking in their usual pemmican suppers. *It's just protein*, Oscar tells himself. His mouth responds with a rush of saliva. Spooning tasty mouthfuls from his cup with enthusiasm, he assesses the others. Amundsen and Helmer are already finishing up their serving with one eye on the pot. Helmer reaches in and skewers a chunk of meat. Amundsen follows suit. Both men gnaw their way through two, three bits, drawing in the cool air of the tent to whisk away the dense heat of the tasty morsels.

'Hey, leave us some,' howls Sverre.

'Chewy,' says Helmer, his mouth full and issuing steam as he speaks.

Amundsen gives a crooked smile as his teeth peel the meat back from a sliver of bone that has found its way into the pot.

Helmer dives in for a fourth time. Bjaaland grabs his sleeve. 'Learn your table manners from the dogs?'

Helmer seems genuinely surprised at the rebuke. 'What's wrong with you?'

'How many bits of meat have you had?'

Sverre uses the opportunity to secure a few cuts for himself. He points to the pot and raises his eyebrows at Oscar in silent invitation.

'Five pieces each,' Oscar says, lifting his cup to his mouth and sucking in the savoury dregs of his first course. The taste lingers pleasantly. His tongue explores every nook and cranny for shreds of meat. Now for the scary part.

'I'm done,' says Amundsen, sitting back and drawing his sleeping bag up around his shoulders. 'If anyone decides he doesn't want his share, I'll help him out.'

Muffled sneers give him an indication of his luck in that department.

Oscar closes his eyes and takes his first bite. Judging it out of ten, Oscar thinks maybe a six would be in order. The meat seems rather tough and in need of salt. It's certainly lacking the kind of melt-in-the-mouth quality he would find appealing in a meat dish back home. But ultimately he must admit it's very satisfying to be chewing something for once. He may yet grow to love it.

CHAPTER FORTY

Just how long this will go on nobody can say for sure, but the roar outside the tent sends a clear message – the blizzard is not ready to release them just yet. It's the fifth day of their confinement. The air is thin at 3000 metres. Helmer complains that even rolling over leaves him breathless with the effort. The temperature has dropped considerably. There is no alternative but to lie in their sleeping bags bored out of their minds. Bjaaland can think of nothing but stretching his skier's legs. Outside, amid the swirling vortex of snow, the remaining dogs sleep off their mammoth feast. Hopefully it will restore their depleted reserves of fat.

They've all railed against the protracted storm. Now it's Sverre's moment to give voice to frustration. 'I'm sick of this tent, I'm sick of sleeping, I'm sick of scribbling in this diary about doing nothing. If I have to lie here another day I'll scream.'

'Yeah, yeah,' Bjaaland says wearily. Rather than turn vocal, he's retreated into his own skin. He learnt his lesson about venting his spleen back on the Axel Heiberg Glacier.

'If we're not first at the pole, we might as well not have left Norway,' continues Sverre.

There's a pause.

'Why don't we just head out,' says Oscar. 'Anything is better than this.'

Bjaaland murmurs in a noncommittal way and steals a glance at Amundsen, who is lying on his back, evidently lost in thought. His breath escapes in even clouds from his sleeping bag and his eyes watch the hypnotic flapping of fabric as the storm sucks at the tent.

'What do you think, chief?' asks Sverre, suddenly cheered by the prospect of action.

'If we all agree, then why not?' Amundsen says without moving. A smile plays about his lips. The men are becoming more like him every day.

The tent is severely iced up. The act of folding could tear it if they don't take great care. Amundsen shouts into the wind like a general as pellets of ice, hard as gravel, break free from the tent and pound his face. Visibility is limited to a few metres. The sledges, buried under mounds of snow after five days, have to be dug out and repacked. Helmer hurriedly builds a depot. All the supplies they can jettison – spare alpine rope, heavy crampons, Sverre's sledge, which is hoisted onto its end – are piled up alongside the rigid carcasses of fourteen dogs.

Finally, Oscar jams a broken ski upright in the snow. It's his silent offering to the ice gods. 'Can't be too careful in this fog,' he says.

Harnessing the reluctant dogs requires serious manhandling and strong language, but before long they are ready to move on, five men and three dog teams, into a ferocious gale. It is nearly impossible to keep their eyes open. The snow is as fine as sand and penetrates every hole and crevice of their clothing. It catches on the fur of their anoraks and hoods and frames their faces in a filigree of frost that soon hardens to armour. Cheeks freeze, the skin becoming candy red before turning hard and white. Noses, chins, jaws succumb to frostbite. Every now and then the men must massage life into the trouble spots with their bare hands, which they hurriedly slip back into reindeer gloves.

Amundsen goes ahead as forerunner. In the whiteout conditions, staying upright is his most pressing challenge.

He might as well be blind. Melted together, the sky and land make a mockery of the world about him. Is he going up or going down? Several times he tips over like a toy soldier. The surface feels gritty; skiing on sand would be easier. Every now and then a break in the clouds allows the sun to reveal utterly alien scenery. Each time they struggle to make sense of it. Are those mountains or is it merely a bank of rising mist? The dogs are not troubled by such concerns. There is only the thrill of being in the harness together. The wide plain offers level ground for their exuberance but even as the terrain shifts downhill, their pace does not alter. Soon they are bounding with unreasonable haste down a steep incline into thick fog.

This is madness. No visibility. Blindly galloping towards some ghastly end – a cliff, a crevasse, a chasm large enough to swallow the lot of them. 'Halt!' Amundsen shouts.

Oscar cries out in alarm, having reached the same conclusion. Helmer and Sverre manage to bring the teams to heel only with extreme skill.

'We go no further today,' Amundsen says to the assembled team. Breathless, each man nods in silent agreement. Making camp on a hillside is far from ideal. Everything will be done on an uncomfortable lean tonight.

That's an important lesson, thinks Amundsen. *We should never give in to our impulses.*

CHAPTER FORTY-ONE

Sleep does not come easily. Altitude is undoubtedly playing havoc with the body's natural rhythms – breathing, digestion. And all the red meat consumed over the last few days is sitting like lead in the gut; Amundsen knows its effect on his haemorrhoids will be pure agony.

This snail's pace is infuriating for the chief. The pole may be within reach but conditions are beyond certain. He hates the fact that the ground is falling away. At 3000 metres they should have done with all of that. They should be on the flat. Already at 86 degrees south and not through the mountains? Amundsen forces himself to concentrate on the four degrees of latitude that remain. Perhaps a week lies between them and Shackleton's world record of 88 degrees, 23 minutes, assuming they maintain their pace. To pass that point would deliver a boost to morale. But the infernal delays imposed by heavy weather, fog, wind drift, a treacherous surface and sticky snow offer the scenario Amundsen most fears – that they will only arrive after Scott.

'Stop your bloody snoring!' Amundsen shouts.

The bodies rearrange themselves. The snoring ceases. It's 3 a.m. Suddenly aware of how much brighter it appears outside through the tent fabric, Amundsen wriggles free of his sleeping bag and slouches over to the flap. He delivers a swift kick to Sverre's sleeping form as the wheezing starts up again, but then realises it's Bjaaland who's responsible for the hideous sounds. He kicks him too.

The dogs look up as Amundsen appears. The chief takes in his surroundings for the first time. In a rare show of generosity, the sun has offered a glimpse of the landscape. Amundsen is dressed lightly. He folds his arms tightly across his chest for warmth and walks a short distance to see what lies beyond the tent. A couple of animals let out an expectant yap. Satisfied that no immediate peril awaits them on their chosen path, he returns to bed. Small careful steps will see them through, day after day after day in this wilderness of white summits and ridges and hillsides and plains. They just need to keep at it. Soon enough they'll reach the Antarctic Plateau proper. They have to.

They break camp by 8 a.m. to face yet another day of obstacles. The route plunges down then up again. It feels like they're conquering a mighty sea one huge frozen wave at a time. The dogs lurch, stagger and scrape their way to the top of each hard-packed drift then stumble down the other side, sinking to their shoulders in the loose snow that has pooled in the hollows between the massive swells. Poor desperate creatures, thinks Amundsen; perhaps they should lighten the loads? A depot of ice-hard snow is hastily erected and a black provision crate placed on top.

Setting off again, the men are thankful for a brief window of sunlight. The panorama would inspire poets. A mountain rises at least 4500 metres into the air and appears topped with a crown of colossal ice crystals. The giant presides over a sea of enormous glaciers which tumble downwards in horrible disarray. The largest of them stretches right across their path as far as the eye can see. Gnarled and violently misshapen, it's like a dragon's tail on an unimaginable scale.

'I've never seen anything like it,' says Amundsen, half in awe, half in dread. 'It looks like someone's lifted the continent above their head and smashed it down in anger.'

'It's old,' says Helmer. 'Look how it's all filled in with snow. There'll be a way through. Sure to be.'

Binoculars reveal a possible approach. Heads together, the men discuss the best way to tackle the task. And then, seemingly on cue, the weather closes in. The monster retreats into the gloom. As if the challenge wasn't great enough already, now they will have to pick out the route from memory.

'Perhaps it's for the best,' Amundsen says, trying to be philosophical in the face of dreadful luck. 'Staring at the immensity of this glacier would put any man off attempting to cross it.'

Sverre and Amundsen rope up and gingerly establish a path between crevasses. Helmer, Bjaaland and Oscar accompany the three dog teams in careful convoy, all too aware that any misstep could be fatal. The dogs proceed with an almost human sense of caution. Last to cross, Oscar feels a sickening thud as the snow bridge collapses under him. The dogs bark. He snatches at his sledge, hauling himself clear of the void. The dogs skitter forward, alarmed by the abrupt jerk and even more by Oscar's panicked cry. Safety by a hair's-breadth. Oscar can't help but look down. The depth of the blue hole makes his guts surge. Instinctively he reaches for the nearest dog and buries his face and both hands into its fur.

'You alright, Oscar?' Helmer calls back.

It takes him a moment to answer. 'Yes,' he says finally.

Meanwhile Sverre and Amundsen have their own challenges.

'How can we go any further? It's pure chaos,' Sverre says with a doleful look on his face.

Amundsen can see for himself the impossibility of their surroundings. 'The Devil's Glacier', they've started calling it. The only rational course is to hold their position.

Amundsen calls to Helmer. 'We're going set up camp. But I need you to come on a scouting mission. Let's find a way through this labyrinth.'

Helmer is weary. He'd prefer to retire to his sleeping bag. But refusing the chief is unthinkable. 'Come on, Helmer,' says Amundsen. 'It's like finding a way through the Northwest Passage all over again.'

'Yeah, nothing to it,' Helmer replies with a sneer. 'Only took us three years.'

With growing frustration, the two men soon realise they must endure 2 kilometres of ducking and weaving between gaps and crevasses to travel a fraction of that distance in the right direction. The wind has whisked away more snow, revealing ancient blue glacial ice. Skis offer limited function on such a slippery surface. And where are the crampons? As fate would have it, abandoned with all the equipment deemed surplus to requirements back at the Butcher's Shop depot. This could spell the end of their journey. The race lost over such a trifle. Amundsen clenches his jaw so hard he thinks it might shatter.

Helmer will not give up. He manages to pick a path, making headway even if it can only be measured in metres, tacking east then west over snow bridges that look set to disintegrate under his weight. Up an incline, slowly down a slope, between pressure ridges thrust up like municipal buildings until it seems they can tend southward again.

'Take a look at that!' he shouts.

A long wall of ice, rising 6 metres or more into the air, blocks their route. Clearly it has been standing guard for some time, judging by the large opening that the wind has carved at its heart.

'If this is the Devil's Glacier then that must be Hell's Gate,' says Amundsen.

The two men establish a pathway and, with a bit of careful sidestepping, manage to look through the hole. They both agree that the going appears better on the other side.

'See? What did I tell you?' says Helmer. 'Nothing to it.'

CHAPTER FORTY-TWO

Back at Framheim, the final preparations are being made for another journey into unknown territory. The exploration of King Edward VII Land lacks the glamour of the polar journey, but it might prove a consolation prize should the main party fail to reach the pole.

Prestrud, Stubberud and Johansen's rudimentary investigations will take them deep into the eastern stretches of the Great Ice Barrier. They're also charged with surveying and mapping the Bay of Whales and its immediate surroundings. Finally, Amundsen has asked that they get on top of hut maintenance. They may need to spend a second winter holed up in Framheim's homely confines. The last request turns out to be the most taxing, and the days are full of chores. Keeping their network of tents and tunnels free of snow is a full-time job, but entirely necessary. The roof of the coal store has already collapsed under the weight of accumulated snow.

In the midst of the hustle and bustle, Johansen has time to reflect on what he considers a most unreasonable punishment. Once they return to Norway, Prestrud and Stubberud will have the excuse of damaged heels to explain their exclusion from the polar journey; Johansen will still be nursing his damaged pride. The disastrous September start is still a sore subject. Nobody seems inclined to discuss it. Johansen does the only thing he can think of to get the weight of his calamitous downfall off his chest – he writes to his wife:

When one is so far away and left to one's self in the great loneliness, one broods about one thing or other . . . For my part, I can still be glad that I have not suffered any injury, but still possess my indomitable strength . . . I did not get to the pole, I naturally would have liked to . . . we did good work. But you know the great public asks who has been to the pole. Well, I don't care. I dare to say that nevertheless I have also helped the Southern Party to reach the pole, even if I couldn't be on the final assault, and I know that I was appreciated by those with whom I worked . . . Ah well, as things are, it has all turned out for the best.

Having written it, he doubts he will ever send the letter. They no longer live together and they certainly never speak. His wife hates him in fact – and with good reason. It is with great shame that he recalls the last time he ever saw her. Blonde hair hanging loose about her face after he tossed a bucket of cold water over her head. He had pushed her outside then and locked the door. It was midwinter. It's a small miracle the poor woman did not freeze to death.

'How many times must I ask you? Clear your things from the table, Hjalmar,' scolds Lindstrøm.

Johansen folds the letter and slips it into his pocket. The others are about to eat supper. Despite Lindstrøm's protestations, he excuses himself and takes a solitary walk to the edge of the sea ice to try and banish the blackest thought that has ever entered his mind. But he knows, one way or another, it will catch up with him.

CHAPTER FORTY-THREE

They are mythic in size, crevasses hundreds of feet across and possibly thousands deep. At least they're easy to spot. In fact the men can't help peering over the side with a sort of stomach-churning glee. *'There but for the grace of God go I,'* they have a fondness for saying. Long skis are three times blessed when crossing treacherous-looking sections of rotten surface; more so when skimming over innocent-looking stretches of pristine snow. Misplaced confidence can crumble in an instant.

'Whoa!' Helmer shouts, pivoting on his heels.

A mighty crust breaks away under the back of his skis

with a dull booming sound, revealing a void that has been waiting a thousand years to swallow a man. This is a land of traps and snares. Not long after, Oscar's dogs disappear into a hole and must be hauled up one at a time, utterly bewildered. Amundsen takes it as a sign to make camp. Ironically, there is solid ice underfoot and they must secure the tent pegs with an axe. Five kilometres of progress, that is all they have to show for their day of hard slog. It's woeful compared to their usual distance. Twice since setting out across the glacier they've decided to take a rest day but then can't resist the temptation of continuing when the latest observation places them ever closer to Shackleton's record. At the crest of every ridge, hope reigns supreme – will their troubles be over? Disappointment and dismay are the answer more often than not. But gradually the nature of the Devil's Glacier is changing. Perhaps the end is in sight.

It is 4 December. Haunted by the threat of the Scott stealing the show, the Norwegians have become battle hardened, acting like a marauding Viking party taking ill winds and dire peril in their stride. And it's not just the weather conspiring against them. This final section of the Devil's Glacier is by far the worst they've encountered.

'Wonderful conditions for a skater,' says Amundsen drily, as he appraises the wide valley of sheet ice.

Apart from Amundsen, who skitters about on his skis, everyone has decided to proceed on foot. Every step sends a bone-rattling shudder through the surface like a dungeon door slamming. It is obviously hollow underneath. If they can shuttle the dogs across quickly enough, it might just hold.

'This must be the Devil's Dancefloor,' someone suggests through gritted teeth.

The dogs' claws scratch and scrape, unable to get purchase on the slick surface. Ultimately much pushing from behind is necessary, but with unexpected results. Oscar's sledge breaks the surface and tips over onto its side, one runner dipping into a crevasse. Sverre is quick to his side. Together they lie with their heads in the hole, discussing the best course of action while Bjaaland calmly gets his camera out and takes a photo.

Oscar eyes the deadly fate he narrowly escaped.

'What does the crevasse look like?' Amundsen yells from the front.

'You know, the usual ... bottomless,' shouts Sverre casually.

How accustomed they've become to danger.

APRIL 1910 – BUNDE FJORD, NORWAY

He's a tall man. It is extremely difficult for him to hide. The dark recess under his heavy desk is just big enough to accommodate his length. He draws his long, thin legs up under his chin and listens. The voices in the next room are muffled. He cannot make out one single word. Not even the language they're speaking.

The door to his study creaks open. 'Roald?'

His brother whispers again. 'Roald, are you there?'

'Under here,' Roald hisses.

'What on earth are you doing under there?' Leon peers at his brother. 'Captain Scott is here. He's in the sitting room with

Tryggve Gran. To see you. Remember I told you he was expected today?'

Roald Amundsen is red in the face, annoyed that his brother has put him in this ridiculous situation. 'Well, he can sit there all he likes. I won't be meeting either of them.'

'But I told you he was coming to see you. He telephoned several weeks ago. He's been to see Nansen. He wants to discuss his plans for the South Pole and to coordinate some scientific experiments with you, while you are at the North Pole. It sounds splendid.'

'That may be, but I shall not be meeting with him. Not today or any other day. I am unavailable.'

Leon groans and gets to his feet. 'I'm not sure what to tell them, Roald.'

'Just get rid of them. I don't have time for this kind of interruption.'

Amundsen winces as the door into the hall clacks behind him. He purses his lips. So Nansen is behind this. Friend, mentor. Forcing a proud Norwegian into the arms of the Englishman, wanting them to be partners in science. He wants everyone to work together for the common good. Explorers don't pair up. The thought is ludicrous. He has his own plans, his own expedition to prepare for. He doesn't have time to be drawn into the plans of others.

Carefully he unfolds himself from under the desk. He sits for a moment, listening. Voices, barely audible through the wall, continue to taunt him. Why doesn't Leon get rid of them?

Years have gone into the preparations, the planning, the provisioning. He's got influential sponsors and a boat. He's got a small party of men signed up for adventure. For months he's toured the United States, Europe and Britain, lecturing on his Northwest Passage adventure to generate publicity and raise cash for wages, equipment, food and fuel to last the five years he's estimated the drift across the North Pole would take him and his crew. Again his eye flits to the copy of the New York Times *on his desk. The headline seems to mock him.*

PEARY DISCOVERS THE NORTH POLE AFTER EIGHT TRIALS IN 23 YEARS

It matters little to Amundsen that his friend Dr Cook also claims to have reached the North Pole first. What matters is the fact that the northern prize is no longer a prize. Who in their right mind would want to finance an expedition to drift across the North Pole on Arctic currents now? After Peary and Cook, Amundsen's planned attempt is pointless.

A minor setback, *Amundsen muses.* Nothing that cannot be overcome. The clothing remains the same, the skills of the men, the ice-breaking capability of the boat, the eagerness of the sledging dogs – why wouldn't I turn my gaze southward? The British don't own Antarctica. And Scott has yet to stamp his name on the South Pole. Why should Scott claim the prize before he has even earned it? Partners in science, Nansen thinks! Scott and I will never be partners. We're rivals. It's just that Scott doesn't know that yet. And what he thinks is his, will certainly be mine.

CHAPTER FORTY-FOUR

It's a fine day for breaking records. For once the surface is perfect in every way. The sun is out. Helmer carries the flagpole on the leading sledge and Amundsen, who has set out in front as usual, instructs him to raise it when the sledge-meter confirms that they have knocked Shackleton off his perch.

For the best part of a day Amundsen suffers the usual monotony associated with being the frontrunner – the lonely tedium of aiming one's skis into the empty land-scape, the impossibility of trying to maintain a straight course into the nothingness with Helmer's constant course

corrections of 'more left' and 'more right' wearing thin –
but then suddenly he hears:

'Halt!'

The resounding cheer from behind brings Amundsen
up sharply. To turn and see the Norwegian flag fluttering
in the sunshine infuses him with intense feelings of pride.
Whether they are tears of joy or of tears of sweet relief
Amundsen isn't sure – he's just happy to hide such uncharacteristic emotion behind dark glasses.

This will be the site of their final depot. Sverre and
Oscar offload 45 kilograms of weight from their sledges
to ease the burden on their faltering dogs, now as skinny
as goats. Hollow-sided, they eat their own excrement and
gnaw the wood of the sledging cases. Bjaaland's are in
even worse shape. He's bitter at being saddled with such
wretched beasts, who struggle even on the flat. If it weren't
for them, he'd have skied to the pole already.

Feeding time is even more a fight for survival than
usual. Madeiro has become a rather desperate individual.
Cheeky and utterly sure of himself, he'll seize any opportunity to snatch what is not his. Naturally a fight breaks out.
A tangled knot of snarling and biting dogs skids across the
snow before petering out near a tent. Yelping and retreat
are followed by a licking of superficial wounds. Cowed by
his mother's savage refusal to share her supper, Madeiro
decides to try his luck elsewhere. Oscar places a reassuring

hand on Camilla's head. She spins around and growls a low warning, her lips curled, teeth bared. Oscar takes a step back. This creature is no longer recognisable.

'We must consider them enemies now,' says Sverre.

'And yet they carry on day after day doing exactly what we ask,' Oscar says.

'Not all of them.' Sverre arches his eyebrows knowingly.

Keen to point out that he's not to blame for the lost dog, Oscar says, 'The chief reckons the Major went off to die in peace.'

'Hope he got some,' Bjaaland calls over as he looks out across the plateau. He marvels at how such vastness can feel claustrophobic. Victory could not come too soon.

The depot is marked using their trusted method of laying pieces of chopped-up sledging cases 5 kilometres to the east and west. They'll continue making cairns every few kilometres just to be sure. Although they are all basking in the glory of having seized Shackleton's record, celebrations have been rather circumspect. Amundsen feels their high spirits are far better employed in maintaining forward momentum. There is a fair chance that Captain Scott has also crossed this symbolic line at 88 degrees, 23 minutes. They'll need to reach the finish line first if they want to secure a world record that cannot be broken.

'Next stop, 90 degrees!' is Helmer's rallying cry as they set off the next day but there's still distance to cover and who knows what the weather has in store for them.

The temperature hangs between minus 15 and minus 30, with a wind chill that lays waste to their faces. Amundsen, Oscar and Helmer spend the evenings examining the dreadful topography of sores and scabs with small mirrors they've brought along for the purpose. Helmer picks at the edges of his frostbitten nose and wonders if a beard wouldn't offer better protection. He decides not to raise the issue; refusing to take part in Amundsen's compulsory Saturday evening shaves might be interpreted by the increasingly tetchy chief as mutiny.

'Count yourself lucky, Helmer,' says Sverre archly. 'If you were in the tropics, you'd be flyblown by now.'

They've been navigating by dead reckoning using compass readings and the sledge-meter. When circumstances allow they make their observations using a sextant to establish the position of the sun, chronometers to pinpoint the exact time, and their navigational tables. It is a minor triumph when both methods are in agreement. They are so close. Perhaps two or three days away. It is a time of excitement and longing. Physical and mental fatigue also. The weeks at altitude are taking a toll.

'You'll get your breath back when we win,' goads Amundsen. They'd all appreciate a fresh set of lungs but the chief is speaking of morale too.

Will Scott be there? Every day each man silently studies the unbroken emptiness for signs of life. But day after day the southern horizon remains blank. Until the evening of 13 December.

They've released the dogs, unloaded their provisions and are struggling against the wind to pitch the tent when Sverre says suddenly, 'Anyone else see those black shapes?'

The shapes are unmoving and probably some distance off, although it's hard to tell with windblown snow causing such problems with depth of perception. Amundsen sees. The British camp? His heart skips a beat. 'Bjaaland!' he calls, his anxiety borne aloft on the spindrift whipped up by the southerly. 'Take a look please.'

Bjaaland straps his skis back on and sets off with the kind of explosive energy only a champion skier could muster so late in the day. However, a mere 20 metres into his mad dash, he stops. Eyes remain glued to him. Not a word is spoken – is this the fearful moment of discovery? The moment when their dreams turn to dust? With his signature loping gait, Bjaaland returns to camp. 'Optical illusion,' he says. 'They're dog turds.'

There are barely 15 kilometres to go. The surface is so flat that they could, in all likelihood, see if a Union Jack was flapping in the distance, asserting its dominance over the South Pole. To point this out seems rather like tempting fate. They've all fallen back on little superstitions.

The tent is silent but for the sibilant whisper of the Primus and the slurping sounds of men enjoying their supper. Food is certainly a comfort for their jangled nerves. After dinner Amundsen lies in his sleeping bag and considers all the things that might have gone wrong for them during the journey from their starting point at the foot of his garden on the Bunde Fjord. There are not many things he would change, if any. He considers his career, the steady progression since he was that fifteen-year-old boy reading of Sir John Franklin's adventures. Whatever he has achieved has been the result of lifelong planning, painstaking preparation and the hardest kind of conscientious work. Teetering on the brink of success, Amundsen enters a strange mental state. Fear and doubt have been constant companions; dread and ambition powerful motivating forces that have driven him on with single-minded focus. To dismiss them outright, to replace them with joy and satisfaction does not feel quite right. Yes, he feels the relief of having almost achieved his aim, and a pleasurable sense of vindication at having planned his assault to perfection, but any delight in victory tomorrow must be tainted with an ill-defined melancholy, like a cloud passing over the sun on a summer's day. The race is virtually over. He records the day's weather and their position in his diary but cannot face writing any solemn words on this eve of making history. Tonight he will keep his own counsel.

CHAPTER FORTY-FIVE

The sun chases itself around the sky like a poor trapped honey bee, never deviating from its course, never dipping its radiant head. This could be the centre of the universe. Helmer knows how close they are. He urges the dogs on into a nasty headwind. In an unexpected break with routine, Amundsen has taken up his position further back in the team, perhaps deeming Helmer's compass and the sledge-meter the only trustworthy judges in this delicate dance to an invisible finish line.

Helmer has not spared the whip; its searing lick of pain has proved a necessary cruelty in this final stage of the journey. The dogs can sense the end, Helmer is sure of it. For days they have appeared slightly perturbed, their snouts raised in quiet investigation whenever gusts of wind come somersaulting at them from the pole. Then again, the animals have grown so attuned to the men's moods that perhaps their behaviour merely mirrors their masters' own furtive longing for the endless trek south to finally be over. He glances at the compass, again to the sledge-meter. *If only I had this blasted wind at my back instead of full in the face,* he thinks.

'What's the matter?' Amundsen's skis glide to a standstill.

'The dogs are skittish,' Helmer says with an offhand tone that disguises true intent. 'Do you mind going out in front? They're all over the place.'

Amundsen frowns. The dogs were positively flying ahead but he trusts Helmer's judgement and it's no strain to return to his role as frontrunner. If anything, it will be a challenge to keep ahead of the pack.

Again they plunge forward on the featureless plain, this time with the assurance that their leader will be first among men. *It is only right*, thinks Helmer.

Their most esteemed leader, a man of steel and will and obsession; Helmer follows in his tracks with a mixture of admiration, trust, and even love swelling in his chest as he considers the extent to which Amundsen has shaped his destiny. He is a man like no other, a personage of such depth and complexity that Helmer doubts he will ever get the full measure of Roald Amundsen.

The wind is unyielding, gnawing at his aching, frost-bitten face as it has for weeks, but the southerly gales are at the very limit of their powers. Helmer savours the sweet thrill of checking the sledge-meter one last time.

'Halt!' he calls.

Amundsen stops. So this is it. The geographic South Pole. How odd to be standing on the spot where nothing but latitude matters, a vanishing point where all lines of longitude cease to exist. It is a realm of absolutes that lies far from the trivial considerations of man, from even notions of good and evil. They shake hands, exchanging smiles and animated sounds but no words. Their feelings are unique and complex, beyond language.

Amundsen assumes a detached air as he takes in a 360-degree sweep. Such a forlorn place, this 90 degrees south, with a character so bland and unassuming as to make their effort and suffering to reach it seem utterly out of proportion.

And where is Scott? His dreaded motor sledges? Not here yet, although there is no doubt in Amundsen's mind that they will get here. Scott is determined and more than capable. Just not quick enough. Helmer extends the ski poles that have been lashed together to serve as a flagpole.

Amundsen invites each man to grasp it in a symbolic gesture – they will plant the Norwegian flag together. It's an expression of his gratitude, communicating succinctly his profound admiration for these heroic men. The story could have ended very differently.

'Thus we plant thee, beloved flag, at the South Pole, and give to the plain on which it lies the name of King Haakon VII Plateau.'

CHAPTER FORTY-SIX

'I miss trees,' says Sverre after supper. 'A hillside of green. You know, the way foliage moves in the breeze. I think that would be the most restful sight for my eyes right now.'

'I miss the smell of damp earth. On a spring morning,' says Oscar, indulging his poetic side. 'When you go for a walk through the forest and that smell sort of engulfs you.' He's spent the evening engraving every item in their possession with the date and the location: Sydpolen – the South Pole.

Bjaaland smiles. 'I want an apple. A crunchy one.'

'I'd love to let everyone in the world know what we've

just done,' Helmer says. 'Our families would be so proud to know where we're celebrating tonight.'

'Well, we're not there yet.' Amundsen raises his eyebrows. 'We'll need all day tomorrow to pinpoint the exact location of the pole. That means measuring the sun's altitude at every hour from six in the morning until seven at night.'

'You're joking!' says Helmer. 'That cheeky bastard practically stays in the same spot all day and night.'

Laughter fills the tent.

Amundsen barely raises a smile. 'That's why our single observation is unreliable and therefore valueless. I want to take the first observation at midnight.'

'Not sure I can help with that technical stuff,' says Bjaaland, yawning. 'My navigational skills are non-existent.'

'Too technical for me too,' says Sverre with a mocking smile.

'Helmer and I will handle that side of things,' says Amundsen. 'I'll give you lot another job.'

Amundsen explains how Oscar, Bjaaland and Sverre will need to ski off in different directions, two at right angles and one continuing their old course across the plain. They'll need to cover a distance of 20 kilometres to be sure that the pole lies within the confines of the large square they will be marking out with flags made from dark fabric, attached to spare sledge runners along with a small bag containing a note giving the position of the Norwegian camp.

'So you're really saying we're not there yet?' Bjaaland sounds deflated.

'We need to be triple sure of hitting the spot.' The explorer's face takes on a serious cast. 'May I remind you of the fiasco when both Peary and Cook claimed to be first at the North Pole?'

Ceding victory to the British over a technicality would be a tragic end to their Antarctic journey. They sit in silence, each contemplating how it would feel to have their victory reduced in the public mind to deception and lies.

'Why wait for morning then? The sun is shining,' says Oscar with enthusiasm he's unsure his colleagues will share. 'We can call supper breakfast, and set out immediately. Put the matter to rest once and for all.'

'Polheim' is the name they give to their newly established camp 10 kilometres on from their original position. Three days of observations are complete. They stand at the South Pole. Bjaaland takes the photo of the silent ceremony, the Norwegian flag set atop their spare tent, which they will leave here to mark their conquest. Inside are a few sundry items, along with a brief note:

Dear Captain Scott

As you probably are the first to reach this area after us, I will ask you kindly to forward this letter to King Haakon VII. If you can use any of the articles left in the tent please do not hesitate to do so. With kind regards I wish you a safe return. Yours truly,

Roald Amundsen

It seems a fair request. Despite their success, there's no guarantee they will get home alive.

Now that their official duties are complete, Helmer must attend to a rather more unpleasant task. There can be little doubt that Helge is spent. Helmer leans over to examine the dog, once such a powerhouse and now hunched up on the snow and refusing all food.

'Helge, my friend,' he says, patting his flank.

Nothing escapes in response save the weakest flutter of breath. Helmer grimaces and brings Helge's life to an end with a swift blow to the skull. There is no justice in feeding a loyal and hardworking dog to the pack, and Helmer feels vile as he divvies up the remains. Within a few hours, there is no proof that Helge made it all the way to the South Pole, beyond a few teeth and the shaggy tip of his tail left on the snow.

CHAPTER FORTY-SEVEN

The Norwegians set a terrific pace with the sun on their faces and, finally, the dreaded southerly wind at their backs. Bjaaland is happy to leave his sledge and act as fore-runner, retracing their old tracks at lightning speed. The others follow as best they can – Helmer and Oscar with two teams of eight dogs, Sverre and Amundsen struggling a little to keep up with the fevered advance into blinding sunlight. Snow goggles offer negligible protection against the glare. Their eyes water and ache.

'Give me some bad weather!' roars Sverre at the sun, shielding his eyes.

They all agree a day of haze or gloom would be pure

bliss. After suffering for a couple of days they opt to travel at night, when the midnight sun is comfortably overhead, casting the briefest of shadows before them as they continue their route north.

The cairns that they erected on the plateau were well worth the minor effort of building them. At only a metre high, they are nonetheless highly visible on the clean-sheet flatness, showing up like miniature beacons emitting a reflective glow. The men still scan the horizon for signs of Scott – as much out of habit as a sort of devilish curiosity – but there is no indication that they will have to share the Antarctic plateau with the members of the British expedition.

Amundsen cannot still his whirring mind, which is drifting dangerously close to paranoia when it comes to Scott. 'He can only be a matter of days from reaching the pole,' he mutters more to himself than to anyone in particular. Despite the favourable conditions, the chief's mood is at its most sombre. For him it's not over. In fact, the real race has just begun.

'It's our story and we must be the ones to tell it. If Scott gets back first, he can cast our victory in whatever light he wishes. It'll be Cook and Peary all over again.' He runs a hand over his ravaged face. 'The newspapers love nothing more than a scandal.'

Once before he lost the upper hand. The memory is still a painful one.

October 1905 – Herschel Island, Yukon

The greatest achievement of his life and Amundsen is frozen in. He has no money and no way to communicate his conquest of the Northwest Passage to the world. Captain Mogg of the whaling ship Bonanza, held fast by the sea ice on Herschel Island, also wants out. He has money and a proposition.

The telegraph office in Eagle, Alaska, lies 800 kilometres away over mountains and through the heavy snows of early winter. Inuit travellers Jimmy and Kappa will guide the two men.

'I'm in charge,' says Mogg, peeling off dirty dollar notes and shoving them under Jimmy's nose. The captain is a lazy, corpulent

man, scarcely capable of walking the length of his ship without wheezing. Their one dog sledge will be his command post – he has paid for it, after all. He will dictate when to stop and when to go, where to camp and when to eat the foul and inadequate baked beans he so foolishly insists on for every meal.

Amundsen runs beside the sledge like a dray horse; it's a wonder Captain Mogg has not fixed him with harness. His mind swims at the hateful situation, at the powerlessness of his position, at the thought of all those cans of pemmican the captain refused that would deliver the kind of energy his body craves.

The Times *of London will pay handsomely for the exclusive story of his Northwest Passage victory. He can settle his debts, pay his men their wages, and escape this crushing financial burden. Through weeks of exhaustion, of deepening snows, of staring at the rubbery-faced Captain Mogg belching by the fireside, of holding his tongue, Amundsen fixes on his goal.*

With considerable relief he sends the telegram to Nansen, who is happy to settle the substantial charges associated with transmitting it. Such stupendous news from the wilds of Alaska. A certain Major Glassford of the US Signals Corps thinks so too. He sees fit to share the message with the local press before it is received in Norway. Turns out The Times *won't pay a penny for Amundsen's account. It is old news, in fact, having already appeared in every American newspaper from San Francisco to New York.*

It's an excruciatingly long 800 kilometres back to Herschel Island to tell his men, even if he no longer has to suffer the odious

Captain Mogg. How the telegram was intercepted, and who can be accused of indiscretion, is largely irrelevant. Only one thing is certain: Roald Amundsen has learnt one of life's most valuable lessons – trust no one.

CHAPTER FORTY-EIGHT

Christmas comes and goes, celebrated with little more than a box of cigars that Bjaaland has hidden in his sleeping bag for months. There's a certain indulgence in allowing thoughts of home and loved ones to invade their tent, but sentimentality does not last long when there are worn-out dogs to sacrifice to the greater good. All three were excellent dogs; all three are consumed in a trice.

The remaining dogs have put on weight. In an unrelenting game of cat and mouse, Bjaaland employs all his skill as a cross-country skier to outrun Helmer's leading sledge. The dogs nip the heels of the champion. Helmer hoots with approval. Oscar has rigged up a sail on his sledge to support the boisterous efforts of his team, which includes powerful pullers Camilla and Madeiro, but he has no hope of taking the lead.

'The dogs are going so well, we could do much more than 15 kilometres a day!' complains Bjaaland after a day of sunshine and flat surface. 'We could double our distances.'

Amundsen won't concede. He's adamant that sixteen hours' rest at this altitude will preserve their energy for the ordeal that lies at the ghastly frayed edge of the Antarctic plateau. Negotiating the Devil's Glacier, this time from the opposite direction, is a distressing prospect.

'My tooth is killing me,' says Oscar, rubbing his swollen cheek.

There'll be no sympathy from the chief. His neck and shoulders ache under an enormous phantom pressure. The Transantarctic Mountains loom on the horizon and nothing about their surroundings looks familiar.

'My tooth is killing me,' complains Oscar again.

Nobody engages.

'Where's the mountain with the crown?' asks Helmer.

Nobody can make it out. Is it possible that the giant has disappeared? Illusory light, a change in perspective, an unfamiliar angle all add to the confusion. But where are they? All trace of their old tracks has disappeared and not since 88 degrees have they set eyes on a cairn.

'Are we lost?' asks Sverre, in a low voice that only the chief will hear.

Amundsen snaps, 'Of course we're not lost. We're heading north, aren't we? That's all we need to know.'

Sverre's reply is less discreet than his original question. 'But we'll overshoot our depot. We need those supplies.'

It's a reasonable observation, one worthy of discussion. But instead Amundsen heaves himself forward, his poles digging into the snow forcefully. He wants rid of Sverre and his troublesome comments.

Referring to his notebook in the tent later on, he's surprised the bearings he took are in such a muddle – probably noted down in haste, under stress – they were facing a crisis on the way up, after all. They may face another on the way down.

'My tooth,' says Oscar, staring into his little handheld mirror. 'I can't go on like this. It's too painful.'

'You're the one who did the dental training, Oscar.'

'You expect me to yank my own rotten tooth out?'

'It can't be very painful then, or you'd just do it,' Helmer goads.

Amundsen looks up from his notebook. 'Where are the forceps?'

There's no mucking about as the chief heats his instrument in the Primus flame. Oscar, kneeling in his sleeping bag, tips his head back. 'Make sure it's the right one,' he quips in last-minute warning.

They're not so much forceps as pliers, capable of exerting huge force on whatever object is grasped in their vice-like jaws. Amundsen considers his task. If he cannot pull the rotten tooth, he will crush it to pieces. Oscar can pick the shards from his gum at leisure.

Oscar groans as the pliers lock around the throbbing tooth. Amundsen's lips form a point as he exerts greater and greater pressure. Oscar does his best to mask the blinding pain but everyone hears the high-pitched creak as soft flesh and bone yield to the pliers' extreme force. Amundsen snarls with determination as his knuckles turn white and both hands quiver with exertion, frustration and rage. 'Got you!' he shouts. The tooth is a yellow nub set in pink and grey pulp.

Oscar cradles his jaw. 'You enjoyed that,' he says in an accusatory tone.

'Any other customers?' Amundsen asks, holding up his hard-won prize.

The others turn away, disgusted.

'At least your bad breath will improve,' says Bjaaland, disappearing into his sleeping bag.

CHAPTER FORTY-NINE

Helmer can't help himself. The fingernail of his index finger tentatively explores the outer edges of his scab, tests it with gentle pressure until tenderness sets his finger roving over his chin in search of something he can flick off. The discussion in the tent continues.

'I wouldn't complain if I were you,' says Oscar mildly. 'We've managed to bypass that awful Devil's Ballroom *and* the Devil's Glacier – we've done in one day what took three days.'

'But we still don't know where we are.' Sverre's face is stern. 'And that depot on the edge of the Devil's Glacier, we have no idea where to find it.'

Bjaaland pipes up. 'We've come too far west. The depot has got to be east of us.'

Amundsen corrects him. 'Our course has tended too far east. The depot lies to our west.'

Bjaaland gives a sullen shrug but chooses not to contradict their leader. Time will tell. Ultimately, does it matter who's right? The weather looks far from promising and the chances of finding the depot are becoming increasingly slim. Rations are sufficient to get them back down to the barrier but the dogs won't last three days. No dogs, no pulling power. Each man's thoughts turn to the man-hauling harnesses they all carry in reserve.

'Shall we carry on to the Butcher's Shop?' Helmer asks the next morning. 'We could spend days looking for this depot and never find a damn thing.'

Amundsen squints towards the mountains. They're sure to recognise some landmark before long. But if they don't? What then? 'Okay,' he says resignedly.

Tending ever northward, they remain committed to their course while feeling ever more unconnected to their surroundings. Heads swivel this way and that, trying to make sense of the peaks and formations that flank their undulating route. It's only when they turn to face south that they figure they must actually be quite close to their original tracks. Nobody could forget that view over the

Devil's Glacier that had so intimidated them on their way south.

'See! We came too far to the west,' Bjaaland says with sudden confidence.

Murmurs of grudging acceptance echo round. But they soon see that angling further east will not get them where they need to be. In fact, they've overshot the Butcher's Shop by some distance.

'We should turn back,' says Amundsen, pursing his lips in annoyance.

Helmer is quick to volunteer. He knows time is running out. Bjaaland also raises a hand.

Amundsen looks unsure. 'I don't like to get separated.'

'Relax,' Helmer says. 'It can't be more than a kilometre or two.'

Amundsen has misgivings. He watches the two men strike out and curses the temptation and trickery of this place, how one moment it can appear magical and miraculous and next distorted and malign, enticing prey into its mouth only to snap it shut. It will be pure torture staying put and waiting this out.

Helmer and Bjaaland travel for some time. Wave over icy wave they battle, Helmer with his dogs hauling an empty sledge, which bucks and kicks in the absence of any ballast, and Bjaaland doing his best to follow on skis. Eight kilometres becomes eleven, then fifteen as the fog closes in and the men struggle through increasingly deep snowdrifts where nothing is as it appears.

'We should have brought sleeping bags at least,' Helmer says, scowling. 'If the weather packs it in, we'll be in trouble.'

Back at camp, Oscar and Sverre have turned in. Amundsen will not rest until he sees his two men return. Eight hours they've been gone – it should have taken them two or three at most. Pacing back and forth, scanning the muddle of pressure ridges to the east through his binoculars, Amundsen feels dread at the deteriorating weather. How could he have let them cast out alone without any shelter? No provisions, nothing to drink? How could he have done otherwise? With their spare tent left at the pole, they only have one. And as for food, hopefully they'll eat something once they locate the Butcher's Shop. Another hour inches by, and another. Amundsen considers their options. In all likelihood they'll need to kill off the remaining dogs and manhaul back to Framheim.

Ten hours have passed when, out of the fog, dark shapes appear. Clutched by sudden euphoria, Amundsen sweeps into the tent and sets to work preparing food and drink for the returning men.

Oscar's head emerges from the sleeping bag. 'Are they back already?'

'Back already? They've been gone ten hours!' scolds Amundsen as he fiddles with the Primus.

Sverre's voice is muffled by the reindeer fur. 'Did they find the depot?'

'Looks like it. Neither of them were riding on the sledge, so it must be quite heavily loaded.'

The pot is soon bubbling away. There is a disturbance outside – dog sounds mostly, but also the laboured breathing of men.

'We're back!' Bjaaland sticks his head in the tent. He pushes his hood back. 'Sixty-seven kilometres.'

'What?' Amundsen is incredulous.

Both Oscar and Sverre are now sitting up in their bags. 'You're joking,' says Sverre.

'No,' says Bjaaland with pride. 'Sixty-seven kilometres in ten hours. I just need to help Helmer with the dogs.'

Amundsen gets to his feet. 'No, Bjaaland. You come in. I'll get Helmer. Leave the dogs to me.' The first thing Amundsen sees on leaving the tent is the forlorn sight of dog carcasses piled high on the sledge. 'Get inside, Helmer, and fill your tank.' He slaps the man on the back.

For once, Helmer has no cocky reply. He's hungry and tired, with a raging thirst that he's desperate to satisfy.

We're safe, Amundsen thinks as he unbuckles the dogs from their traces. *But we came so close to disaster.* He shakes his head. Gratitude is a funny emotion, one that he does not often have cause to experience in its full flush. But he feels it now.

CHAPTER FIFTY

Spirits are high. Fog, snowfall, gales and thick cloud have all tried to waylay progress, but with little effect on morale. Amundsen has twice increased their rations over the past weeks. And there's plenty more food in the depots up ahead. They gorge themselves at every meal, clear in the knowledge that any man eating double rations is helping to reduce the weight of the sledges. It's an odd turn of events; there's never been any excess to offer. Satisfied to the point where his guts ache, Bjaaland has to rub his belly in order to sleep. It seems like they have entered a new golden era where they will put on weight rather than lose it.

They are well into their descent of the Axel Heiberg Glacier, enjoying the exhilaration of skiing down the slopes that had so taxed them on their journey south. The long skis aren't designed to turn, even for a champion skier like Bjaaland, and there are a few spectacular crashes along the way. Even the crevasses fail to strike fear in the hearts of men who, not so long ago, exercised such caution. Recent days have seen them steer around any obstacle or pitfall at speed, yahooing with little regard for personal safety. The two dog drivers watch the fun with a hefty dose of envy – they'd far rather be testing their technique than facing the stress and strain of getting the dog sledges down in one piece.

Down on the barrier once again, Amundsen glowers. A nasty thought has just occurred to him, one that increases his sense of urgency. The Norwegian route up the Axel Heiberg Glacier was short and steep but enjoyed the massive advantage of being a whole degree of latitude closer to the pole by the time they hit the high-altitude plateau. The Beardmore Glacier by comparison may have disadvantaged the British by forcing them onto the oxygen-deprived atmosphere of the plateau earlier than the Norwegians, but coming down again Captain Scott and his men will benefit from the relative ease and speed of a longer descent and find themselves out on the barrier more than 100 kilometres closer to their base.

'What time is it?' asks Sverre.

'Six.'

'What day is it?'

'No idea.'

'I know it's 1912,' says Bjaaland, yawning.

They laugh.

Sverre restates his original question: 'So is it six in the morning or at night?'

'Does it really matter?' Amundsen asks.

Perennial daylight makes keeping conventional hours a pointless exercise; a rhythm of eating, sleeping and skiing marks their progress. That said, time is all they think about. A speedy return is once again their single unifying focus.

Has the *Fram* arrived to collect them? It's already the second week of January. Amundsen was clear in his instructions to Captain Nilsen – make haste. That assumes nothing untoward has happened either to the ship or the crew. So many unknowns could still unseat their well-laid plans.

Warmer temperatures greet them closer to the coast. Minus 8 degrees feels tropical compared to the hard white prison of minus 50, but it is not cause for celebration. The heavy snow that falls on them melts on contact before turning to ice. It clings to the dogs' fur, encasing their bodies in a semi-transparent carapace that splinters like candy when the harnesses are strapped tight.

'Well, look who's here!' says Oscar, pointing with his ski pole at two skua gulls playing a lazy game of tag against a sky feathered with clouds.

'They're far from home,' marvels Helmer. 'The sea must be more than 350 kilometres away.'

The seabirds are the only life they've seen in months. Goodness only knows what they survive on in this wasteland, where lonely eddies of ancient snow twist like ghosts from the surface of the barrier.

'No doubt Lindstrøm would see it as a sign,' says Amundsen a little wistfully.

'Favourable, I hope,' says Sverre.

Bjaaland celebrates with two shots of his rifle. Neither bird falls from the sky. He swears. It would have been great to eat something other than pemmican and dog.

There are other signs of life as they approach 82 degrees. It's almost like coming home, laying eyes on this depot, the last one they managed to lay in the autumn. How remote its location had seemed when they first set it up, like the last outpost of civilisation. Now it seems far from civilised. Boxes have been dragged off, upturned, gnawed open and emptied of much of their contents. The two carcasses that were slung atop the depot have disappeared without a trace. Judging by the paw prints, a marauding band of dogs has been through here in recent days. But from where? Could it be the dogs that went missing from Framheim over winter? It's an intriguing thought.

Familiarity boosts confidence. Nothing can blacken their mood. They've made the journey to 82 degrees so many times before that this final stage of their journey home would feel like a backyard dawdle were it not for the atrocious weather. The line of flags spaced out at 1-kilometre intervals offers a surprising degree of comfort when the weather presses in and visibility is reduced. The dark flags troop forward like a marching band, announcing the men's victorious arrival home with the rhythmic beating of fabric in the wind.

CHAPTER FIFTY-ONE

Lindstrøm loves nothing more than a grand parade. The city positively ripples with bunting and streamers. Leaning from windows, children wave Norwegian flags while the hands of parents clutch them tight. A crowd, twenty deep, lines the street. The sound of cheering travels in hypnotic waves across the park and unites with the church bells, which ring out in celebration. Lindstrøm cranes his neck to see the action but his gaze is intercepted by the gentle sway of spring leaves in the oak trees. So green – he has never seen a more exquisite colour. Another cheer rises from the crowd. Now he sees what all the fuss was about. It is a magnificent marching band, its imminent arrival announced by the thump, thump, thump of the big bass drum.

Lindstrøm's eyes flicker open momentarily. He buries his head in the pillow, desperate to catch the tail of his dream before it escapes. Thump, thump, thump-thump. *Ha-ha, got you,* he thinks, snuggling deeper under his blanket.

Heavy boots sound on the wooden floor.

'Good morning, my dear Lindstrøm. Have you any coffee for us?'

Such a familiar voice. Lindstrøm's eyes flick open at the sound of it.

Stubberud is first out of his bunk. 'Welcome,' he says, rubbing his eyes.

'Good God, is it you?' Lindstrøm stares from his bunk, for a moment confused by this early morning arrival, more than a week ahead of schedule. Despite it being 4 a.m., and despite being robbed of two hours of sleep, he is quick to offer some sorely needed hospitality.

Prestrud appears, then Johansen. A slightly awkward reunion ensues – handshaking that quickly turns to bear-hugging, laughter and wild slapping on shoulders and backs. Finally somebody asks the question: 'Have you been there?'

'Yes, we have been there,' is the reply that sends everyone into a renewed frenzy of bear-hugging and back-slapping.

Stubberud hands Bjaaland a creased newspaper and gestures excitedly at the date. 'Feel like reading what's been happening in the real world?'

Bjaaland grasps the paper in both hands, his blood-shot eyes widening with disbelief.

'We've been reading all about the scandal we caused back in Norway,' says Stubberud with a grin. 'Quite nice to make headlines.'

'We're going to make even bigger headlines now,' Helmer says.

'So the *Fram*'s back then,' says Amundsen as he wriggles out of his reindeer skins.

'Arrived on the ninth of January,' Lindstrøm calls from the kitchen.

Prestrud can't resist telling them, 'And there's the oddest little band of Japanese men in a tent down on the sea ice. Their leader's a fellow named Shirase. Says he wants to make a dash to the pole – can you believe that?'

Amundsen frowns. 'Well, I must tell him not to bother – we've checked it out and there's absolutely nothing there to justify such a fool's errand.'

CHAPTER FIFTY-TWO

The door to the chartroom is closed. Captain Nilsen and Amundsen have much to discuss. A stack of mail tied neatly with twine awaits the explorer's attention on the table, along with a year's worth of newspapers – another indulgence to savour in the weeks ahead. Much has happened since they turned their backs on the outside world. Finally, Nilsen asks the question that has hovered in the air between them since the first moments of their reunion.

'Naturally, you've been to the South Pole?'

'Ninety-nine days, a distance of almost 3000 kilometres.'

Captain Nilsen whistles in admiration.

The two men stare at the map on the chartroom table. The same one Nilsen unfurled before the stunned crew way back in October 1910, when Amundsen revealed his true intentions.

'I must admit, I did have my concerns,' Amundsen says with surprising candour.

'Well, covering a distance like that, anything could happen,' Nilsen agrees.

Amundsen gives a snort. 'There was never any doubt in my mind that *we'd* succeed. I was concerned about you and your challenges. Getting to Buenos Aires. Securing the necessary funds.' His eyes bulge comically. 'And coming back here to get us!'

Nilsen assumes a philosophical air. 'Don Pedro Christophersen – that's who we need to thank. He answered our prayers.'

'Well, there's a mountain with his name on it. And . . . one for you also.'

'You're joking.' Nilsen's face is transformed by an enormous grin.

'Actually not a mountain, more a plateau at around 86 degrees south. Sort of around here.' Amundsen swirls his index finger above an empty spot to the left of where the Axel Heiberg Glacier would butt up against the Antarctic Plateau, had any of it been marked on the largely blank map.

Nilsen puffs out his chest. 'How very grand.'

'Mount Olav Bjaaland, Mount Sverre Hassel, Mount Oscar Wisting, Mount Helmer Hansen. You're in good company,' Amundsen says with genuine warmth.

There's a knock on the door. It's Lieutenant Gjertsen, sporting a wild beard and dirty overalls. Despite not being the least impressed by his slovenly appearance, Amundsen accepts the generosity of his congratulatory handshake. He can tell the lieutenant is desperate to hear every last detail of their journey. He and Lieutenant Prestrud will have their heads together for hours.

'Sir,' he says to Nilsen. 'When should we expect the others?'

'Right away, I think.' Nilsen looks to Amundsen for confirmation.

Amundsen nods. 'They've started packing up Framheim already. I've instructed them to take anything of value. The rest they can leave. Half a dozen sledge-loads of supplies at most.'

'Make the necessary space available, Gjertsen, and ready the crew. We're going to have a very busy few days.'

Once Gjertsen leaves, Amundsen fixes his friend with a stern gaze. 'We have to leave here as quickly as possible. I want to be the one to report the news to the world.'

'So I should set a course to Lyttelton? It's the closest port.'

'New Zealand?' Amundsen eyes flash and he shakes his head. 'No. That's Scott's patch. We won't be welcome there. Make for Hobart.'

'Hobart, Tasmania eh? I'm not so sure you'll get a warm welcome there either. Those British colonies . . .' Nilsen's voice drifts off. 'I'm afraid you're not a very popular man, Roald.'

Amundsen's nostrils flare as he breathes in deeply.

'Even in Norway.' Nilsen shakes his head. 'People were bent out of shape over what you did. Parliament wanted to order you home.'

Amundsen huffs. 'Which the king refused to do!'

Nilsen sighs. 'Diplomatically it has been awkward. With the British, I mean. Especially after we had such strong support from them for Norwegian independence. It's a bit of a slap in the face, to be honest, to beat their man to the South Pole. It's been viewed as a breach of "etiquette".'

'Are those people mad? Is the quest for the pole exclusively given to Scott to achieve?' Amundsen's suddenly riled. 'I couldn't care less what they think, those idiots.'

Nilsen forces a smile. 'Nice to have support where it matters though. From what I heard from Don Pedro, Nansen calmed them all down.'

'Yes. It appears so. He understands. And we have the confidence of the King of Norway. And Don Pedro of course. When everyone turned their backs on me, they extend their hands. I owe them more than I can ever say.'

Over the next two days, sledges trundle back and forth to the edge of the sea ice with an odd assortment of clothing and equipment, items of sentimental value and those deemed too expensive to abandon. Framheim, their haven of warmth and companionship, is mostly empty. Lindstrøm packs away a few favoured items into a crate – his lucky ladle, the cursed handheld coffee grinder, the clock-work acrobat with an old woman's face that provided him with such amusement on countless evenings alone in the hut. Pots and frying pan, buckets, mops, plates and cutlery, the trusty coal range – they will all stay.

Towards the end of the day, Amundsen's flustered face appears at the door. 'Time's up, Fatty.'

Lindstrøm nods. He's looked over the odds and ends that remain in the dug-out pantry around the side of the hut. It's a jumbled mess down there and he decides against going through every single can and jar of preserves. He tucks two wheels of Dutch smoked cheese under each arm and heads for the door. However, there is one last thing he would like to do before sealing up their home and setting sail.

There is a pleasing smell of carbolic soap within the hut. Back and forth, back and forth he guides his trusty mop, making sure to chase its foamy head of string into all the corners. The table and chairs have been scrubbed and the mattresses have been dragged outside and beaten soundly in the sunshine. Satisfied that he has left everything in order, Lindstrøm closes the door behind him. He hesitates a moment, keen to fasten the door somehow, but there's no key and no lock. He sighs in resignation. After battling their way to the bottom of the globe, those Japanese are welcome to anything they might find here.

While the others are loading the ship, Oscar goes in search of the captain. He's a hard man to pin down. Twice Oscar has called to him on deck only to have Nilsen raise a hand for patience. More than once he's said, *I'll be with you shortly*, only to disappear below decks.

Oscar knocks firmly on the captain's cabin door.

'What is it?'

'It's Oscar. Permission to enter?'

Nilsen turns wearily from his desk. Whatever the issue, he hopes it will be quickly resolved. His door swings open but it's not Oscar, it's a black and white mass of fur. A dog's wet snout collects his chin, licks his ear. A large head squeezes itself under his hands in wild greeting. Papers fly as dog paws land on the captain's desk and a sniffing investigation gets underway.

'Madeiro?' he says incredulously.

Oscar's head appears around the door, beaming. 'Recognise this mutt?'

'Not sure I would have,' says Nilsen, who is now standing with his arms over his head while the dog leaps about him. 'He's a good deal larger than when I last saw him.'

'Come here,' Oscar growls, grabbing at the dog in an effort to subdue his exuberance. 'Made it to the pole and back. With his mother, Camilla, you remember?'

'I do,' says Nilsen a little reservedly, his hands still above his head.

'Well, just thought I'd let you know.' Oscar yanks the dog towards the door. 'They're all on deck now – all thirty-nine of them – if you want to say hello.'

'Good for you, Madeiro.' Nilsen gives the dog's head a tentative pat; nothing too enthusiastic, he doesn't want to encourage more jumping. *How like the others he's become,* the captain thinks. *Huge, out of control and oh, so smelly!* He looks at Oscar. 'Not quite pet material, is he?'

Oscar laughs. 'No! And he doesn't need your protection anymore. In fact, if I'm not mistaken, I think *he's* pregnant.'

It's 10 p.m. on 30 January when the *Fram* finally motors away from the mooring it so briefly occupied on the edge of the Bay of Whales. Lindstrøm points to where the

Framheim hut would be, if visibility weren't so poor. None of the others have had a chance to say goodbye, deprived of a last glimpse of their cherished home by the arrival of a thick bank of fog. There are mixed emotions up on deck as nine men contemplate their year on the ice. Nobody says anything. No words are necessary.

Finally, Bjaaland turns his back on the scene of whiteness. He leans his elbows on the railing and sets his ravaged face northward. 'Good riddance,' is his laconic send-off.

EPILOGUE

Nothing remains of 'Framheim', Roald Amundsen's Antarctic base on the Ross Ice Shelf, formerly known as the Great Ice Barrier. It has completely and utterly disappeared. Amundsen's Framheim was never meant to be a permanent home, or an enduring monument to the Norwegian explorer's astonishing achievement. Amundsen was in Antarctica to achieve one thing, and one thing only – to be the first man to reach the southernmost point on the planet.

The ice was thick where the Norwegians built their winter hut in the summer of 1911. Amundsen's men dug deep into the ice, carving out a series of underground rooms connected by tunnels so they could move about freely even as the fiercest Antarctic blizzards raged overhead. But the Ross Ice Shelf does not stand still. This great floating plate of ice, locked in the frozen embrace of the Antarctic continent and fed continually by the mighty glaciers squeezing forth from the interior, is prone to breaking off in huge chunks. Gone is Amundsen's simple hut, the sledges, the underground rooms, the ghosts of the Norwegians' restless dogs. In May 2000, whatever remained of Framheim fell into the sea.

If he were alive, Amundsen would shrug his shoulders. 'Good thing we were not having breakfast at the time,' he might reply.

Having secured his victory at the South Pole, Amundsen up and left. No sentimental tears, no regrets. He was pleased to leave the windswept plains of Antarctica for his next big adventure – whatever that might be. Besides, the world was waiting for news. His news.

Three months later in Hobart, Amundsen was able to successfully send word of his achievement to Fridtjof Nansen and the King of Norway. After dodging the clamouring questions of the Tasmanian newsmen desperate for a scoop, Amundsen was able to honour his agreement with the *New York Times, Daily Chronicle* and *London Times* for exclusive rights to his story, thanks in large part to the efforts of his brother Leon in negotiating them.

Short of cash, Amundsen set out immediately on a lecture tour of Australia and New Zealand. Everybody wanted to hear the story first hand of how a band of Norwegian adventurers had so expertly married the best of Inuit and Scandinavian cultures to claim the last continent on earth. Dogs, sledges and skis – there wasn't much more to tell. From Hobart, the men headed home. All except Hjalmar Johansen, who had taken to drink, become quarrelsome and been ordered from the ship to make his own way home to Norway. Shortly after, he took his own life.

As for the dogs, they were thankfully spared another unpleasant sea voyage. A gift was made of them to another expedition that was soon to leave Hobart for Antarctica. The Australian explorer Douglas Mawson was infinitely grateful to the Norwegians. As it turned out, the gift was literally life-saving when dire circumstances compelled him to eat some of their number to survive. Having endured his ordeal, Mawson was able to return a national hero, along with many of Amundsen's original contingent, who lived out their remaining days in far from unpleasant conditions in Tasmania.

Despite his success, the name Amundsen has often been overshadowed by the tragic story of another great Antarctic explorer, Robert Falcon Scott, who died on his way back from the South Pole, in second place. It's true that Amundsen's story may not be as moving as Scott's, but it is difficult not to find the Norwegian explorer an extremely compelling character. Secretive and stubborn, prepared to mislead his colleagues and consume his dogs if it helped him achieve his aims, Amundsen could be viewed in a less than favourable light. But the truth is far more complex and far more interesting.

It's fair to say Roald Amundsen was not the most popular man in Great Britain once his Antarctic achievement was reported in the press. Even less so when news of Captain Scott's death on the ice reached the world the following year. The British public was scandalised. Had Amundsen indirectly caused the death of their national hero by forcing Scott and his men into a race for the pole?

Nobody knows if Amundsen ever spent much time pondering the tragedy and any role he might have unwittingly played in it. We do know he considered Scott 'a splendid sportsman and a great explorer'. We also know that Amundsen was never interested in basking in the glory of his achievement with parades, parties and public addresses, although these things were necessary for a man who desperately needed others to support his endeavours. For him, success meant money. Not personal riches, but funds to finance his next expedition.

Amundsen was no amateur. He was a professional, with no shortage of men to follow him to the ends of the earth. Signing up to one of his expeditions meant hardship, extreme cold, deprivation, possibly death, along with adventure in the company of one of the world's greatest explorers. Being associated with Amundsen would set a man up for life and preserve his name in the rich history of polar exploration. Amundsen's many achievements will never crumble into the sea like Framheim. His achievements are now set in stone. This is the story of but one.

BIBLIOGRAPHY

Amundsen, Roald, *The Roald Amundsen Diaries: The South Pole Expedition 1910–12*, Fram Museum Oslo, 2010

—— *The North West Passage*, Archibald Constable & Company Limited, London, 1908

—— *The South Pole: An Account of the Norwegian Antarctic Expedition in the Fram, 1910–1912*, Keedick, 1913

—— *My Life as an Explorer*, Doubleday, 1927

Bown, Stephen R, *The Last Viking – The Life of Roald Amundsen*, Da Capo Press, 2013

Hanssen, Helmer, *Voyages of a Modern Viking*, George Routledge & Sons Ltd, London, 1936

Huntford, Roland, *Scott and Amundsen – The Last Place on Earth*, Abacus, 1979

Kløver, Geir O, ed. *Roald Amundsen and the Exploration of the Northwest Passage*, Fram Museum Oslo, 2008

——*Cold Recall: Reflections of a Polar Explorer*, Fram Museum Oslo, 2009

——*Antarctic Pioneers: The Voyage of the Belgica 1897–1899*, Fram Museum Oslo, 2010

Ledingham, Rod, *The ANARE Antarctic Dog Driver's Manual*, 2016

ACKNOWLEDGEMENTS

It was tremendous fun writing this book. My research took me to Norway and Tasmania and gave me an excuse to find out about wild locations I hope one day to visit in real life. I'll get to Gjoa Haven yet! While in Oslo I was granted access to the unpublished English translations of the expedition diaries of Hjalmar Johansen, Kristian Prestrud, Olav Bjaaland, Sverre Hassel and Captain Thorvald Nilsen. I am very grateful to Geir Kløver, the director of the *Fram Museum*, for his generous assistance in this regard. It was such a privilege to get a sense of these thoroughly regular guys who achieved wholly extraordinary things.

To find myself aboard the *Fram*, to set foot below decks and let my imagination loose was utterly sublime. And how fortunate to access the fascinating resources within the museum's collection covering all of Roald Amundsen's many remarkable journeys. What a extravagant pleasure for an Amundsen enthusiast hungry to learn so much more.

While in Tasmania I had the good fortune to meet Rod Ledingham who has been travelling to Antarctica since 1966. Rod's excellent book, *The ANARE Antarctic Dog Driver's Manual*, filled gaps in my research with practical advice drawn from Rod's many years' experience working with sledge dogs in Antarctica. It's a great shame I could not share more of the fascinating detail contained within this volume around sledge lashings and knots, the fashioning of whips from seal skin, and how to make a raft from sledge boxes and tent poles when floating out to sea with your dogs on an ice floe. The era of sledge dogs in Antarctica may be over but hopefully I'll find an opportunity to weave Rod's sledging wisdom into another tale!

Heartfelt thanks to my early readers Helen Cunningham and Hilary Stichbury; my wonderful editor Kate Whitfield who knows just when to add and when to cut; my illustrator Sarah Lippett who, despite being terrifically busy with her own second book, was happy to take on Amundsen and his ninety-seven dogs; and to Andrew

Lumsden (aka Te Radar) for sharing such enthusiasm for Amundsen and lending support to my other Antarctic ambitions.

Pawel, my life's companion, must be credited with constantly pushing me beyond the limits of what I consider possible and into the realm of 'what could be' – not an easy task. It is inspiring (and certainly frightening) to be with someone whose work ethic, energy and commitment to excellence would challenge Roald Amundsen himself! Thank you for a colourful life full of spontaneity, love and laughs.

And to my two beautiful boys, Kazimierz and Zygmunt: I hope you can see the simple truth at the heart of this story – life is what you make it.

ABOUT THE AUTHOR

Joanna Grochowicz's narrative non-fiction is meticulously researched and compellingly told. By fusing the real and the imagined in her stories of early Antarctic exploration, she reveals the human aspirations and tragedies that have shaped our understanding of what remains an utterly inhuman place. As an Antarctic writer and communicator, Joanna believes strongly that engaging with Antarctic history encourages a deeper connection with a globally significant continent that few will ever visit. While focusing on polar exploration, her ever-popular school sessions guide students in examining the continued importance of resilience, perseverance and curiosity in all human endeavours.

INTO THE
WHITE

SCOTT'S ANTARCTIC
ODYSSEY

JOANNA GROCHOWICZ